W9-CAA-791

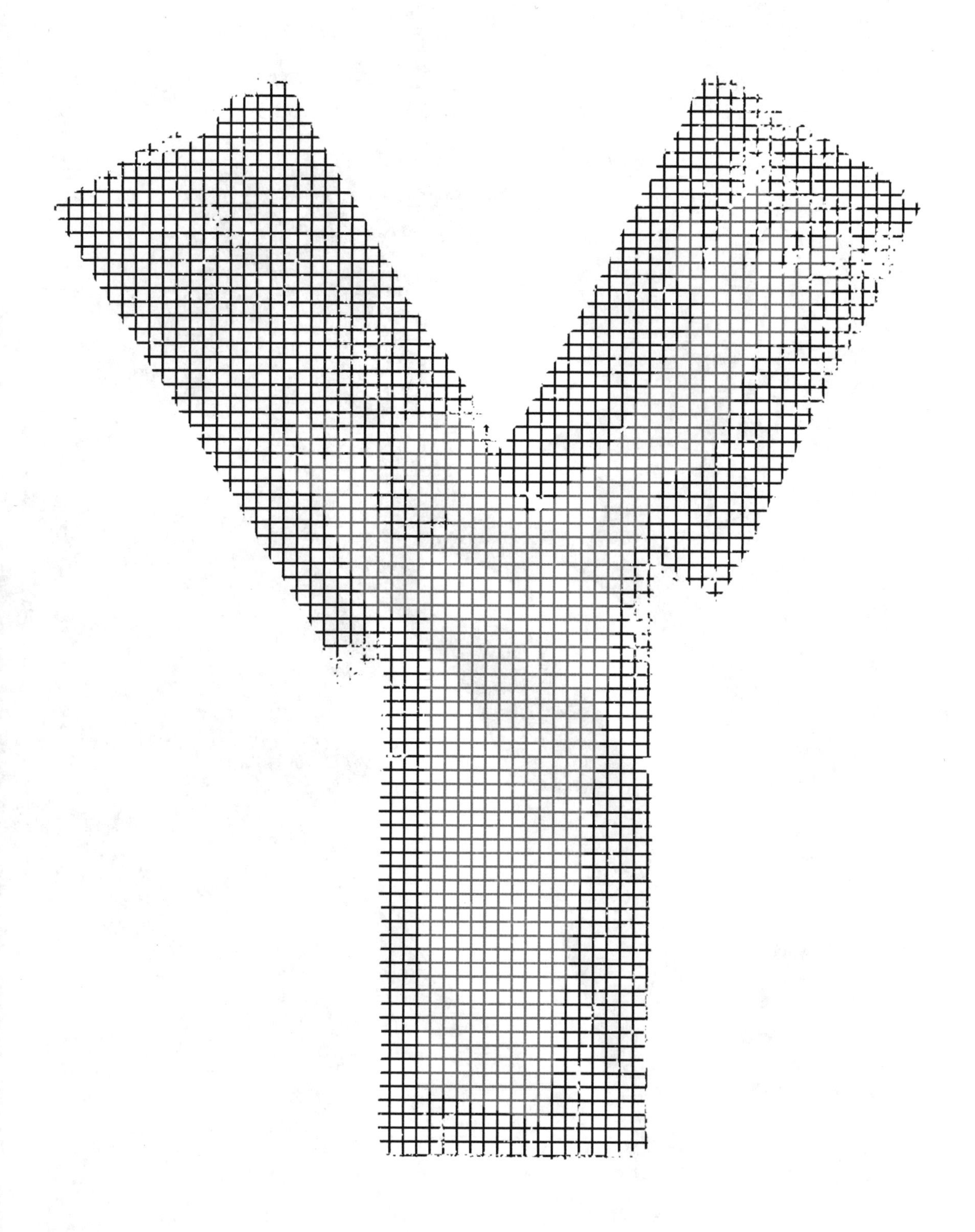

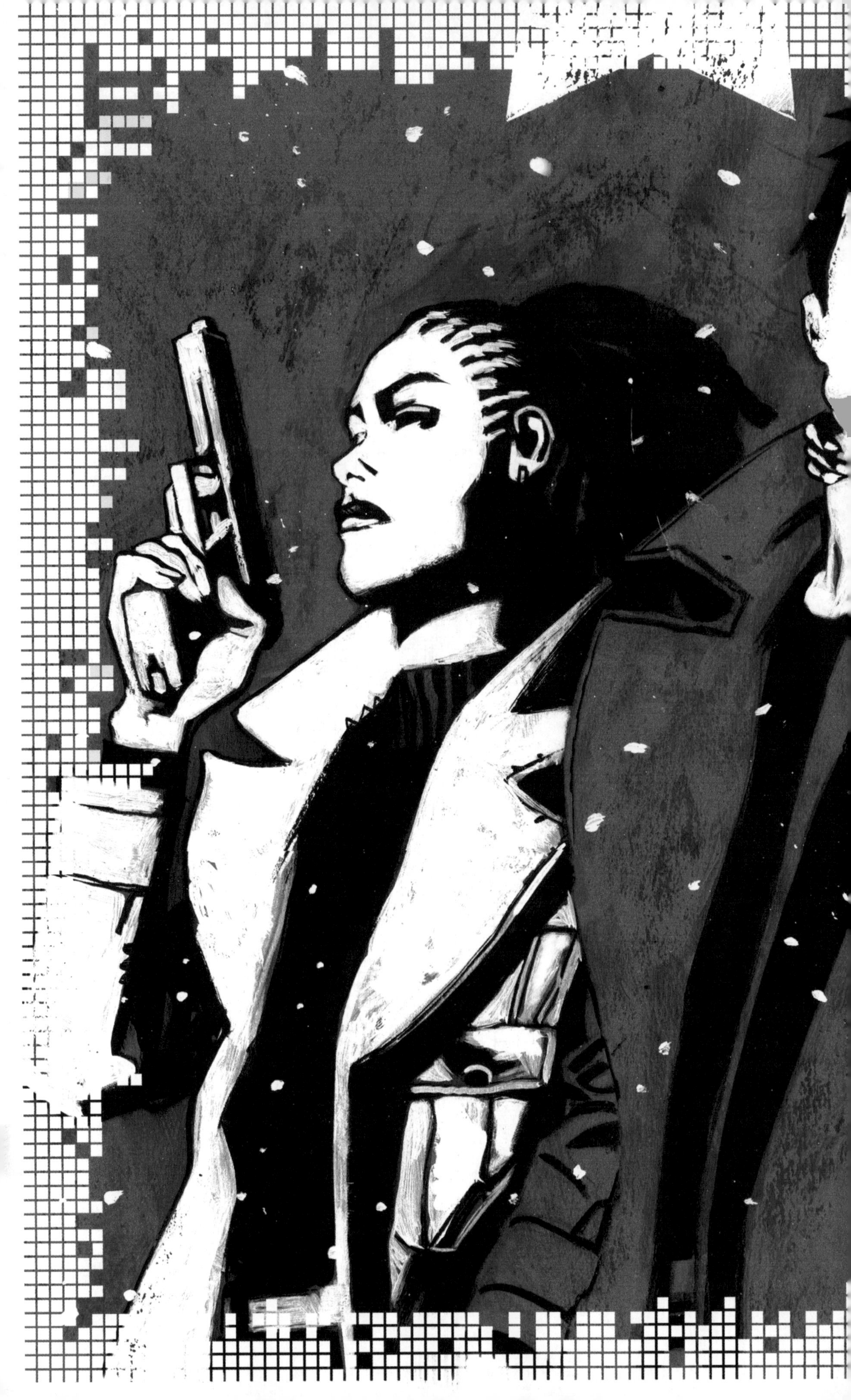

# Y: THE LAST MAN

## The Deluxe Edition

## Book Five

Brian K. Vaughan Writer
Pia Guerra, Goran Sudžuka Pencillers
José Marzán, Jr., Goran Sudžuka Inkers
Zylonol Colorist
Clem Robins Letterer
Massimo Carnevale Cover Art and Original Series Covers
Y: THE LAST MAN created by Brian K. Vaughan and Pia Guerra

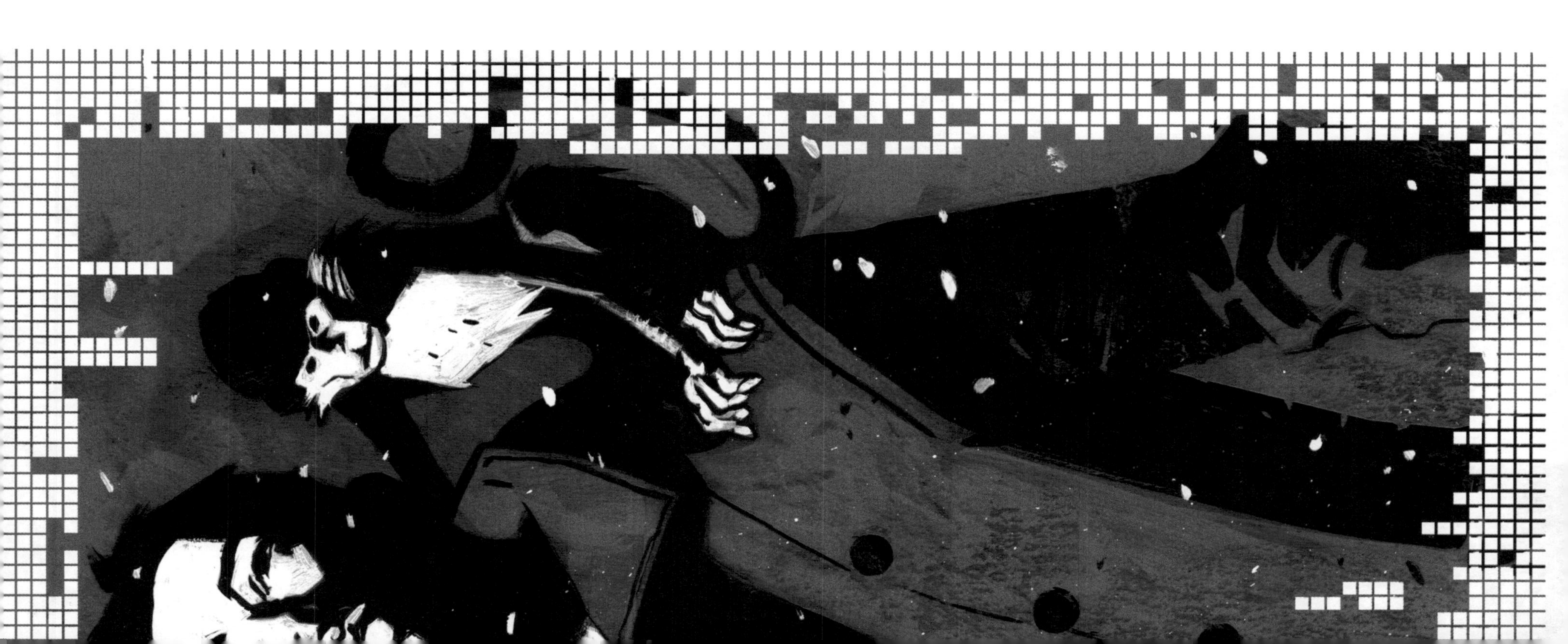

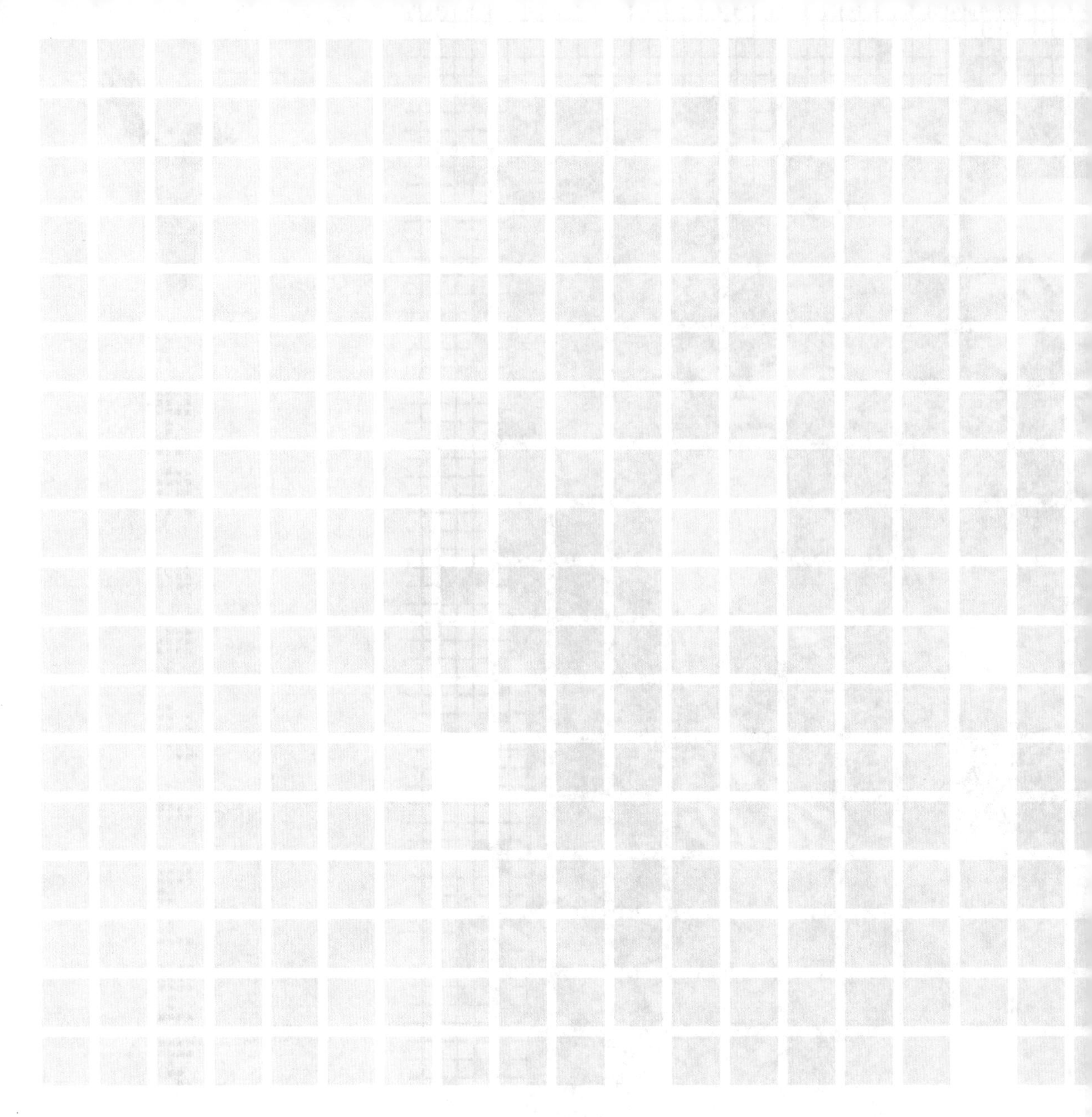

Will Dennis Editor – Original Series
Casey Seijas Assistant Editor – Original Series
Scott Nybakken Editor
Robbin Brosterman Design Director – Books
Louis Prandi Publication Design

Hank Kanalz Senior VP – Vertigo & Integrated Publishing

Diane Nelson President
Dan DiDio and Jim Lee Co-Publishers
Geoff Johns Chief Creative Officer
John Rood Executive VP – Sales, Marketing & Business Development
Amy Genkins Senior VP – Business & Legal Affairs
Nairi Gardiner Senior VP – Finance
Jeff Boison VP – Publishing Planning
Mark Chiarello VP – Art Direction & Design
John Cunningham VP – Marketing
Terri Cunningham VP – Editorial Administration
Alison Gill Senior VP – Manufacturing & Operations
Jay Kogan VP – Business & Legal Affairs, Publishing
Jack Mahan VP – Business Affairs, Talent
Nick Napolitano VP – Manufacturing Administration
Sue Pohja VP – Book Sales
Courtney Simmons Senior VP – Publicity
Bob Wayne Senior VP – Sales

Logo design by Terry Marks.

Y: THE LAST MAN — THE DELUXE EDITION BOOK FIVE

Published by DC Comics.


DC Comics, 1700 Broadway, New York, NY 10019
A Warner Bros. Entertainment Company.
Printed in the USA.
Third Printing.
ISBN: 978-1-4012-3051-7

Library of Congress Cataloging-in-Publication Data

Vaughan, Brian K., author.
Y, The last man. The deluxe edition, Book five / Brian K. Vaughan, Pia Guerra, José Marzán, Jr., Goran Sudzuka.
pages cm
"Originally published in single magazine form as Y: The Last Man 49-60."
ISBN 978-1-4012-3051-7
1. Graphic novels. I. Guerra, Pia, illustrator. II. Marzán, José, illustrator. III. Sudzuka, Goran, illustrator. IV. Title.
PN6728.Y2V48 2013
741.5'973–dc23

2013010228

SUSTAINABLE FORESTRY INITIATIVE
Certified Sourcing
www.sfiprogram.org
SFI-01042
APPLIES TO TEXT STOCK ONLY

Y: THE LAST MAN — Contents

I'M COMING FOR YOU, BETH!

AND I'M COMING HARD!

YORICK?
BETH?
WHERE ARE YOU, DOLLFACE?

ONE STEP AHEAD OF YOU.
SAME AS ALWAYS.

YOU'RE ALIVE!
BUT YOU WON'T BE, UNLESS YOU TURN AROUND AND WALK AWAY.
WHAT THE HELL ARE YOU GOING ON ABOUT?

I'VE BEEN TRYING TO TELL YOU, SOMETHING AIN'T RIGHT WITH ME.

SOMETHING IN MY GRAY MATTER.

NOTHING MATTERS!
EXCEPT THAT I NEED YOU!
THAT'S THE PROBLEM, 'RICK!

THAT'S NOT WHAT YOU CALL ME!
WHY ARE YOU CALLING ME THAT?!

I'M SORRY!
BUT WE'LL NEVER HAVE PARIS...

MMN...?
EEff

EEEEFF
PIPE DOWN, AMPERSAND. WHAT ARE YOU...?

OH, BONNY'S FLINGING HER CRAP AT YOU AGAIN? WASN'T SHE JUST GROOMING YOUR ASS HALF AN HOUR AGO?
HST
SORRY, LITTLE MAN. MIXED MESSAGES ARE THE BANE OF MY EXISTENCE, TOO.
SHE'S FLIRTING WITH HIM, DUMMY.

IT'S CALLED PLAYING HARD TO GET.

ROSE!
HOW LONG HAVE YOU BEEN UP AND AROUND? I MEAN, YOU WERE IN SLEEPING BEAUTY MODE FOR **WEEKS.**
WHAT...WHAT **HAPPENED?**

YOU SERIOUSLY DON'T REMEMBER?
DR. MANN SAID YOU GOT DICED BY THAT **NINJITSU BITCH.** BUT ONCE SHE REALIZED YOU GUYS DIDN'T KNOW WHERE MY MONKEY WAS, SHE BOLTED.

I'LL HAVE TO TAKE HER WORD FOR IT. LAST THING I REMEMBER IS WATCHING SIX INCHES OF STEEL COME POKING OUT OF MY WASHBOARD.
YOU EVER **SEEN** ANYTHING THIS HIDEOUS?

OVER THE LAST FOUR YEARS?
MANY, MANY TIMES.

LOOKS LIKE YOU FINALLY FOUND YOUR PET THOUGH, EH?
YEAH, BUT NOT HIS LIBIDO. THE PHRASE "HOT MONKEY SEX" IS PROVING TO BE FRUSTRATINGLY INACCURATE.
THESE TWO HAVE YET TO MAKE A LOVE CONNECTION, AND UNLESS AMP DROPS A PAYLOAD IN BONNY FAST, I'M GOING TO LOSE HIM. AGAIN.

MAYBE IT'S THE DRUGS, BUT I HAVE NO IDEA WHAT YOU JUST SAID.

DR. MANN NEEDS AMPERSAND TO MAKE MORE INOCULATION FOR THE NEXT GENERATION OF DUDES SHE'S HOPEFULLY GOING TO ENGINEER.
BUT SHE THINKS AMP MIGHT BE ABLE TO PASS WHATEVER ANTI-PLAGUE STUFF IS INSIDE HIM ONTO HIS OFFSPRING. SO IF BONNY CAN GET HERSELF IMPREGNATED, I CAN LEAVE HER WITH MRS. WIZARD AND TAKE AMPERSAND WITH ME.
TAKE HIM WITH YOU WHERE?

THE DOC WANTS TO PRESS ON TO SOME HONG KONG LAB WHERE SHE CAN FINISH HER CLONING WORK, BUT AGENT 355 AND I ARE HEADING TO BEIJING TO CATCH THE NEXT TRANS-SIBERIAN TRAIN TO FRANCE. SO I CAN FIND BETH.
HOPEFULLY, I GUESS.

YOU MEAN, WE'RE... SPLITTING UP?

WELL, I'M SURE MANN WILL WANT YOU TO TAG ALONG WITH HER, BUT MY PART IN THIS WHOLE SCIENCE EXPERIMENT IS PRETTY MUCH OVER.
TIME FOR THIS BLOKE TO RECONNECT WITH HIS SHEILA.
YOUR AUSTRALIAN ACCENT IS WORSE THAN THAT FAKE GIRL VOICE YOU USE WHEN YOU'RE DISGUISED.
SO WHEN DO WE LEAVE FOR CHINA?
LEAVE? ROSE, WE GOT HERE A FEW DAYS AGO.
MANN FOUND THIS COOL SAFEHOUSE FOR US TO REGROUP AT. THE UPSIDE OF LOSING HALF YOUR COUNTRY'S POPULATION IS THAT THE REAL ESTATE MARKET TOTALLY OPENS UP.
SO WE'RE ALREADY DONE WITH JAPAN? HOLY GOD, I DIDN'T PASS THROUGH THIS MANY PORTS WHEN I WAS A FUCKIN' SAILOR.
YEAH, I'VE KEPT MY WATCH ON EAST COAST TIME EVER SINCE I LEFT BROOKLYN. ONLY WAY TO STOP THE JETLAG FROM DESTROYING YOUR--
YORICK, I...I REALLY HAVE TO TALK WITH ALLISON.
'COURSE.
SHE AND THREE-FIFTY SHOULD BE BACK FROM THEIR SHOPPING SPREE SOON. THEY'RE BUYING A FEW THINGS FOR MY "GOING-AWAY DINNER."
WHICH SOUNDS A LOT NICER THAN LAST SUPPER.

**Shenzhen, China**
**Now**

ALLISON, AS MY PRIMARY CAREGIVER, IT'S YOUR RESPONSIBILITY TO PLEASE MAKE ME STOP EATING DUMPLINGS.
TALK ABOUT TABLES TURNING. BEFORE THE PLAGUE, CHINA HAD THE GREATEST GENDER IMBALANCE IN THE WORLD. 120 BOYS FOR EVERY 100 GIRLS.
BECAUSE OF THE ONE-CHILD POLICY, RIGHT? COUPLES ***ABORTING*** THEIR GIRLS TO MAKE SURE THEIR ONLY KID WOULD BE A ***SON?***
THIS PLACE WAS ON THE CUSP OF MASSIVE CRIME WAVES AND HUGE SOCIAL UNREST--ALWAYS HAPPENS WHENEVER THERE ARE SIGNIFICANTLY MORE GUYS THAN GALS.
SO YOU THINK THE PLAGUE WAS ***GOOD*** FOR THESE WOMEN?

IT'S NOT ABOUT GOOD OR BAD.
IT'S ABOUT GETTING BACK TO **EQUILIBRIUM.**

SPEAKING OF WHICH, I WAS HOPING YOU AND I COULD TALK MORE ABOUT WHAT HAPPENED IN YOKOGATA.
YOU SAID THAT AFTER TOYOTA GUTTED ROSE AND STABBED YOU, SHE JUST **DISAPPEARED.** WHY DO YOU THINK SHE LET YOU LIVE?
I DON'T KNOW, I'M NOT A **PHILOSOPHER.**

ALLISON, YOU AND I MADE A PACT BACK IN QUEENSBROOK.
NO MORE LIES.

...
FINE. IT **WASN'T** THAT MASKED ASSHOLE WHO ATTACKED ROSE, ALL RIGHT? IT WAS MY **MOTHER.**

BUT IT WAS AN ACCIDENT.
WE SPOOKED HER, AND SHE...SHE **OVERREACTED.** BUT SHE'S A BRILLIANT SURGEON. MOM'S THE ONE WHO PUT ROSE BACK TOGETHER AGAIN.
AND THEN SHE JUST **ABANDONED** HER OWN DAUGHTER? NO, THERE'S SOME-THING YOU'RE NOT TELLING ME.

WE PROMISED NEVER TO LIE TO EACH OTHER, BUT THAT DOESN'T MEAN WE'RE NOT ENTITLED TO OUR SECRETS, "AGENT 355."

LOOK, IF YOUR MOM IS IN SOME KIND OF TROUBLE, YORICK AND I CAN POSTPONE OUR TRIP.
ROSE IS IN NO CONDITION TO PROTECT YOU.
ACTUALLY, ROSE ISN'T COMING WITH ME EITHER. AS SOON AS SHE'S HEALTHY ENOUGH TO GO BACK TO SYDNEY ON HER OWN, I'M GOING TO LEAVE HER.

BUT I THOUGHT YOU TWO WERE...
AND LIKE EVERY WOMAN I'VE EVER SLEPT WITH, ROSE HAS BEEN LESS THAN FORTHCOMING ABOUT HER INTENTIONS.
WHILE SHE WAS DELIRIOUS, SHE ADMITTED THAT SHE JOINED OUR CREW UNDER ORDERS FROM THE AUSTRALIAN MILITARY. SHE'S BEEN SPYING ON US FOR HER SUPERIORS.

WHAT?
YEAH, I WAS NAIVE ENOUGH TO BELIEVE ROSE CAME WITH US BECAUSE SHE HAD FEELINGS FOR ME.
I'M GLAD TO HAVE IT OFF MY CHEST, ACTUALLY. I CAN'T TELL YOU HOW HARD IT'S BEEN TO--

HAVE YOU LOST YOUR FUCKING MIND?

YOU LEFT THE LAST MAN ON EARTH ALONE WITH A FOREIGN AGENT?
WHAT WAS I SUPPOSED TO DO, EUTHANIZE HER? IF ROSE WANTED TO HURT ANY OF US, SHE COULD HAVE DONE IT AGES AGO.
SHE PROBABLY JUST WANTS TO KEEP TABS ON YORICK'S WHEREABOUTS FOR HER COUNTRY, SOMETHING SHE'LL NEVER DO AGAIN IF YOU LET ME HANDLE HER.

WE HAVE TO GET BACK TO THE HOUSE!
WAIT!
YOU SAID IT YOURSELF, ROSE IS IN NO CONDITION TO--

NNN!

PLEASE, NO.
NOT YET...

New York, New York
Now

HEY! VLAD'S DAD MAY HAVE BEEN A COSMONAUT, BUT HE'S MY SON, NATALYA, NOT RUSSIA'S!
THIS IS MY FAULT, CIBA.
IT'S BEEN YEARS SINCE ANYONE GAVE BIRTH, SO I'M AFRAID BETH, JR. HERE IS PROBABLY THE ONE WHO ATTRACTED ALL OUR UNWANTED ATTENTION.
SISTERS, THEIR STEAMER IS LEAVING FOR EUROPE!
IF THOSE WOMYN TRULY HAVE THE LAST GRAIL OF TESTOSTERONE, WE HAVE TO DESTROY IT BEFORE IT LEAVES OUR SHORES!
I HELP US OUTRUNNING AND ELUDING ENTIRE FATHER-FUCKING ARMY OF ISRAEL, AND YOU LET US FALL INTO TRAP OF STUPID GIRLS WITH ARROWS AND BOWS?
I THOUGHT THE DAUGHTERS OF THE AMAZON WERE IN THEIR LAST THROES!
FIGURES THE DEAD-ENDERS WOULD ALL WIND UP HERE. THE CRAZIES ALWAYS FIND THEIR WAY TO NYC.
<SMART PLAN STATIONING SCOUTS AT ALL THE DOCKS.>
<I FOUND THEM, ALTER.>

YORICK?

YEAH, THAT'S IT. HARDER... FASTER.
'RICK?

SO CLOSE, DON'T STOP!
UM, IS EVERYTHING ALL RIGHT IN HERE?

'EVENING, AGENT.
EEEF
QUIET, THREE-FIFTY.
AMPERSAND'S GETTING HIS CHERRY POPPED!

HE AND BONNY FINALLY...?
ROSE COAXED THEM INTO IT. SHE'S LIKE AN EROTIC MONKEY WHISPERER.
AT THIS CLIP, THE GIRL CHIMP SHOULD BE BANGED UP IN NO TIME.

AND YOU? HOW ARE YOU...FEELING?
ON THE MEND, THANKS TO ALI. IS SHE BACK YET?
SHE'S, UH, STILL PICKING UP A FEW MORE INGREDIENTS.

WELL, YOU'RE A SIGHT FOR SORE EYE.
CAN'T TELL YOU HOW MUCH I'VE MISSED THE SOOTHING CLACKING OF YOUR KNITTING NEEDLES, MATE.

YEAH, THERE'S A LOT I'VE MISSED ABOUT YOU.

...AND THEN WHEN WE WERE CAMPING ON THIS RESERVATION IN NEW MEXICO, I GOT KIDNAPPED BY A BUNCH OF NATIVE AMERICAN WOMEN WHO THOUGHT I WAS A SPIRIT GOD OR SOMETHING.
THANKFULLY, DR. MANN CONVINCED THEM I WAS JUST A HERMAPHRODITE.
ACTUALLY, I SAID YOU WERE A WOMAN WITH A RARE FORM OF **TURNER SYNDROME** THAT ENCOMPASSED A NUMBER OF CHROMOSOMAL ABNORMALITIES.

YOU KNOW, MY HILARIOUS ANECDOTES ABOUT OUR PAST ARE A LOT MORE HILARIOUS WHEN **YOU'RE** NOT HERE.

I WON'T BE AROUND TO BURDEN YOU MUCH LONGER, YORICK.
I'M JUST BUSTING BALLS, DOC. YOU KNOW I'M GONNA MISS YOU LIKE A LIMB, RIGHT?
I SUPPOSE.
THAT'S NORMALLY THE PART WHERE YOU SAY HOW MUCH YOU'RE GOING TO MISS **ME.**

YOU'LL BE HARD TO MISS WHEN I'M SPENDING EVERY WAKING HOUR TRYING TO **CLONE** YOU.

UM, CAN YOU SAY THAT AFTER I HAVE A DRINK? SO I HAVE TIME FOR AN APPROPRIATE SPIT-TAKE?
ALLISON, PERHAPS WE SHOULD WAIT TO DISCUSS SENSITIVE PLANS LIKE THIS UNTIL--

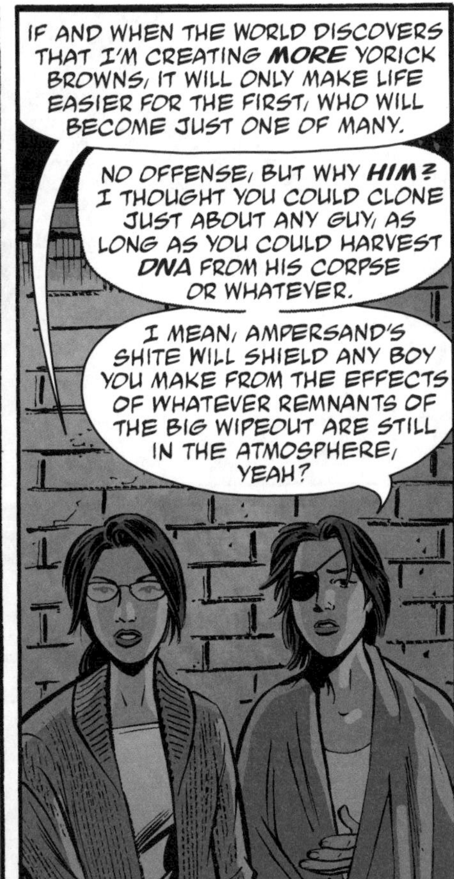
IF AND WHEN THE WORLD DISCOVERS THAT I'M CREATING MORE YORICK BROWNS, IT WILL ONLY MAKE LIFE EASIER FOR THE FIRST, WHO WILL BECOME JUST ONE OF MANY.
NO OFFENSE, BUT WHY HIM? I THOUGHT YOU COULD CLONE JUST ABOUT ANY GUY, AS LONG AS YOU COULD HARVEST DNA FROM HIS CORPSE OR WHATEVER.
I MEAN, AMPERSAND'S SHITE WILL SHIELD ANY BOY YOU MAKE FROM THE EFFECTS OF WHATEVER REMNANTS OF THE BIG WIPEOUT ARE STILL IN THE ATMOSPHERE, YEAH?

THEORETICALLY, BUT I HAVE NO PROOF THAT THE MONKEY'S FECES WILL WORK ON EVERY MALE.
YORICK MAY HAVE A UNIQUE GENETIC MAKEUP THAT REACTS TO AMPERSAND'S ANTIBODIES IN A PARTICULAR WAY.

SO IN THE FUTURE, MANKIND IS GOING TO BE MADE UP ENTIRELY OF ME'S?
IT'S AN ABOMINATION OF SCIENCE! OF GRAMMAR!

I'M ONLY STARTING WITH YOU.
IF AND WHEN YOUR LINE OF DUPLICATES IS SUCCESSFUL, THEN I'LL GET TO WORK RESURRECTING AL GORE AND JOHNNY DEPP.
HOW MANY DIFFERENT...MODELS WILL YOU NEED TO BRING BACK BEFORE HUMANS CAN START REPOPULATING WITHOUT YOUR HELP?

GENETIC BOTTLENECK ISN'T MY AREA OF EXPERTISE, BUT I IMAGINE WE'LL NEED AT LEAST TWO HUNDRED SUBJECTS TO CREATE ENOUGH DIVERSITY TO LIMIT INBREEDING AND FORM AN EFFECTIVE FOUNDER POPULATION.
SO THAT MEANS I'LL EVENTUALLY BE THE GRANDFATHER OF, LIKE, POINT-FIVE-PERCENT OF EVERY MALE ON THE *PLANET?*

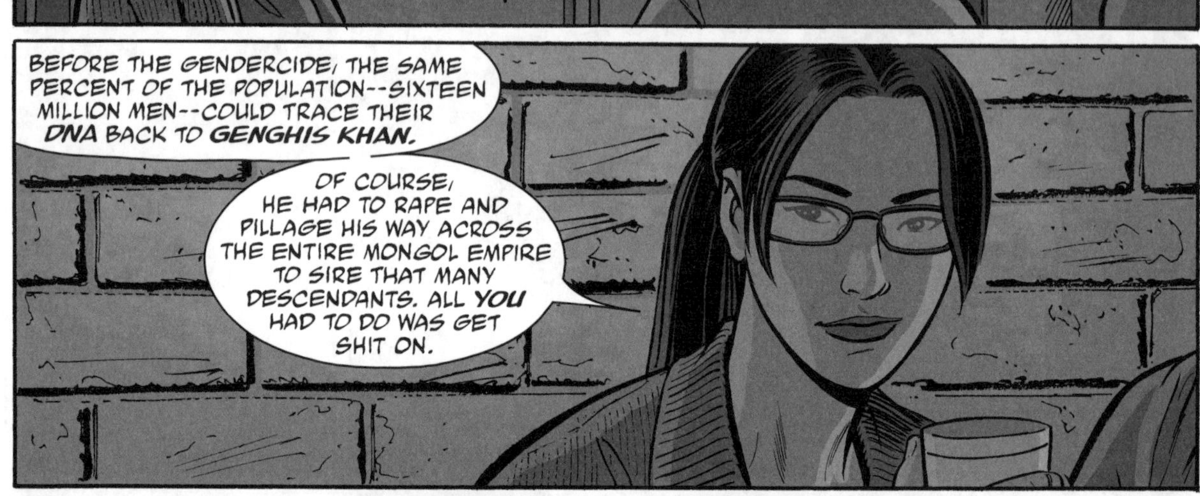
BEFORE THE GENDERCIDE, THE SAME PERCENT OF THE POPULATION--SIXTEEN MILLION MEN--COULD TRACE THEIR ***DNA*** BACK TO ***GENGHIS KHAN.***
OF COURSE, HE HAD TO RAPE AND PILLAGE HIS WAY ACROSS THE ENTIRE MONGOL EMPIRE TO SIRE THAT MANY DESCENDANTS. ALL ***YOU*** HAD TO DO WAS GET SHIT ON.

AND ON THAT NOTE, I SHOULD PROBABLY RETIRE TO MY SICKBED FOR A FEW MORE HOURS.
PROMISE TO WAKE ME BEFORE YOU GO-GO, LAST MATE?
AYE-AYE, SKIP.

CARE TO JOIN ME, LOVE?
AH, IN A FEW, ROSE.
THE OLD TRIO STILL HAS A FEW LOOSE ENDS TO WRAP UP.

NO HURRY...BUT WE HAVE A LOT OF CATCHING UP TO DO.

WHERE THE BLOODY HELL HAVE YOU BEEN?

I NEARLY DIED, CAPTAIN BELLEVILLE.
BUT THESE PEOPLE RISKED THEIR LIVES TO SAVE MINE... UNLIKE THE ROYAL NAVY THAT TIME I WAS ONBOARD THE WHALE.
LIEUTENANT COPEN, NEED I REMIND YOU THAT YOU SWORE AN OATH?

YEAH, TO DEFEND MY HOMELAND.
AND THE BEST WAY WE CAN DO THAT IS TO STOP WORRYING WHAT'S HAPPENING OUTSIDE OUR BORDERS, AND START CONCENTRATING ON WHAT'S HAPPENING INSIDE.
ROSE, WE HAVE A RESPONSIBILITY TO LOOK AFTER THIS MAN'S WELL-BEING. PLEASE, JUST GIVE ME YOUR COORDINATES.

MY COORDINATES ARE AY, DOUBLE-YOU, OH, EL.
GOODBYE, CAPTAIN. ADVANCE AUSTRALIA FAIR.

ROSE?

ALLISON.
I SWEAR, I... I WAS GOING TO TELL YOU.
NO, YOU WEREN'T. BUT WHEN YOU STARTED TO CATCH ON THAT I KNEW, YOU DECIDED TO STAGE THIS LITTLE PERFORMANCE, RIGHT? TO CONVINCE ME YOU'RE REALLY ON MY SIDE?

I DIDN'T THROW AWAY MY OLD LIFE AS A STUNT!
I DID IT BECAUSE I FUCKING LOVE YOU!

AND I SUPPOSE YOU'RE NOT JUST PRETENDING TO BE GAY?
DO I MAKE LOVE LIKE A STRAIGHT GIRL?
HOW MANY TIMES DID I GO DOWN ON YOU OUR FIRST NIGHT TOGETHER?

YEAH, WELL, YOU KNOW WHAT THEY SAY ABOUT CHINESE FOOD.

I'M NOT LYING TO YOU, ALLISON MANN.
I CAN'T.
I...I DON'T CARE IF YOU'RE TELLING THE TRUTH ANYMORE. JUST KEEP SAYING EXACTLY WHAT YOU'RE... YOU'RE...

NAHH!

ALI, WHAT...?
OH CHRIST, YOU'RE BLEEDING.
I'M SORRY, I'M SICK AND I...I DON'T HAVE LONG.

YOU HAVE TO GO...TO A PLACE CALLED... THE BIOETHICS INSTITUTE.
THERE'S A DOCTOR...NAMED MING THERE. SHE STUDIES...MORPHO-GENETIC FIELDS AND...

AND I THINK...SHE KNOWS...WHAT CAUSED...
ALLISON?

DOC?
ALLISON!

WHAT HAVE YOU DONE?
MOTHERLAND

Yokogata, Japan
Twenty-five Years Ago

⟨I CAN HANDLE MY DAUGHTER FROM HERE.⟩

⟨AS YOU PLEASE, **DOCTOR** MATSUMORI.⟩
⟨I'M SICK OF GETTING **SHOTS,** DAD.⟩

⟨I THOUGHT YOU WERE SICK OF BEING **ALLERGIC** TO EVERY PLANT THAT'S EVER BLOSSOMED. WE'RE TRYING TO **HELP** YOU, AYUKO.⟩
⟨BUT I HAVE **HOME-WORK!**⟩
⟨WAIT TO DO IT UNTIL JUST BEFORE YOUR BED-TIME, **AFTER** YOUR CLASSMATES HAVE COMPLETED THE ASSIGNMENT.⟩

⟨WHY?⟩
⟨LET'S NOT HAVE THIS CONVERSATION AGAIN, MING.⟩

⟨IT'S MORE SIMPLE TO GRASP THAN YOUR FATHER SUGGESTS, LITTLE ONE.⟩
⟨IT'S ALL ABOUT **MONKEYS.**⟩

‹A FEW YEARS AGO, A GROUP OF SCIENTISTS WERE STUDYING JAPANESE MACAQUES ON THE ISLAND OF KOSHIMA.›
‹ONE OF THE PRIMATES THEY WERE OBSERVING LEARNED TO CLEAN DIRT OFF SWEET POTATOES BY WASHING THEM IN THE SEA, A SKILL HE SOON TAUGHT TO OTHER MACAQUES.›
‹SWEET POTATOES MAKE MY TONGUE PUFF UP.›

‹BE THAT AS IT MAY, THIS NEW TECHNIQUE WAS QUICKLY ADAPTED BY THE MONKEY'S ENTIRE TROOP.›
‹AND BY THE TIME ONE HUNDRED OF THE ANIMALS LEARNED TO WASH THEIR FOOD, SOMETHING EXTRAORDINARY HAPPENED...THE PRACTICE SPREAD TO MONKEYS ON TAKASAKIYAMA.›
‹ANOTHER ISLAND? HOW? DID ONE OF THE MONKEYS SWIM THERE?›

‹NO, AYUKO. IT'S CALLED MORPHIC RESONANCE, THE SOCIO-BIOLOGICAL INTERCONNECTEDNESS OF SPECIES.›
‹THIS SPONTANEOUS TRANSMISSION OF DATA AT A GENETIC LEVEL EXPLAINS SUDDEN MASSIVE LEAPS FORWARD IN SCIENCE, IN TECHNOLOGY, IN EVOLUTION.›

‹IT MEANS OUR GENES ARE RECEIVERS CAPABLE OF TRANSMITTING AND OBTAINING INFORMATION THROUGH THE UNSEEN "FREQUENCY" THAT UNITES ALL LIFE ON THIS PLANET, LIKE THE INVISIBLE BOND THAT HOLDS TOGETHER ATOMS OF A MOLECULE.›
‹IT MEANS THAT HOMEWORK IS EASIER TO DO IN THE EVENING BECAUSE YOUR FELLOW PUPILS WILL HAVE ALREADY RAISED THE COLLECTIVE CONSCIOUSNESS WE'VE COME TO THINK OF AS "INSTINCT."›

‹THAT'S STUPID.›

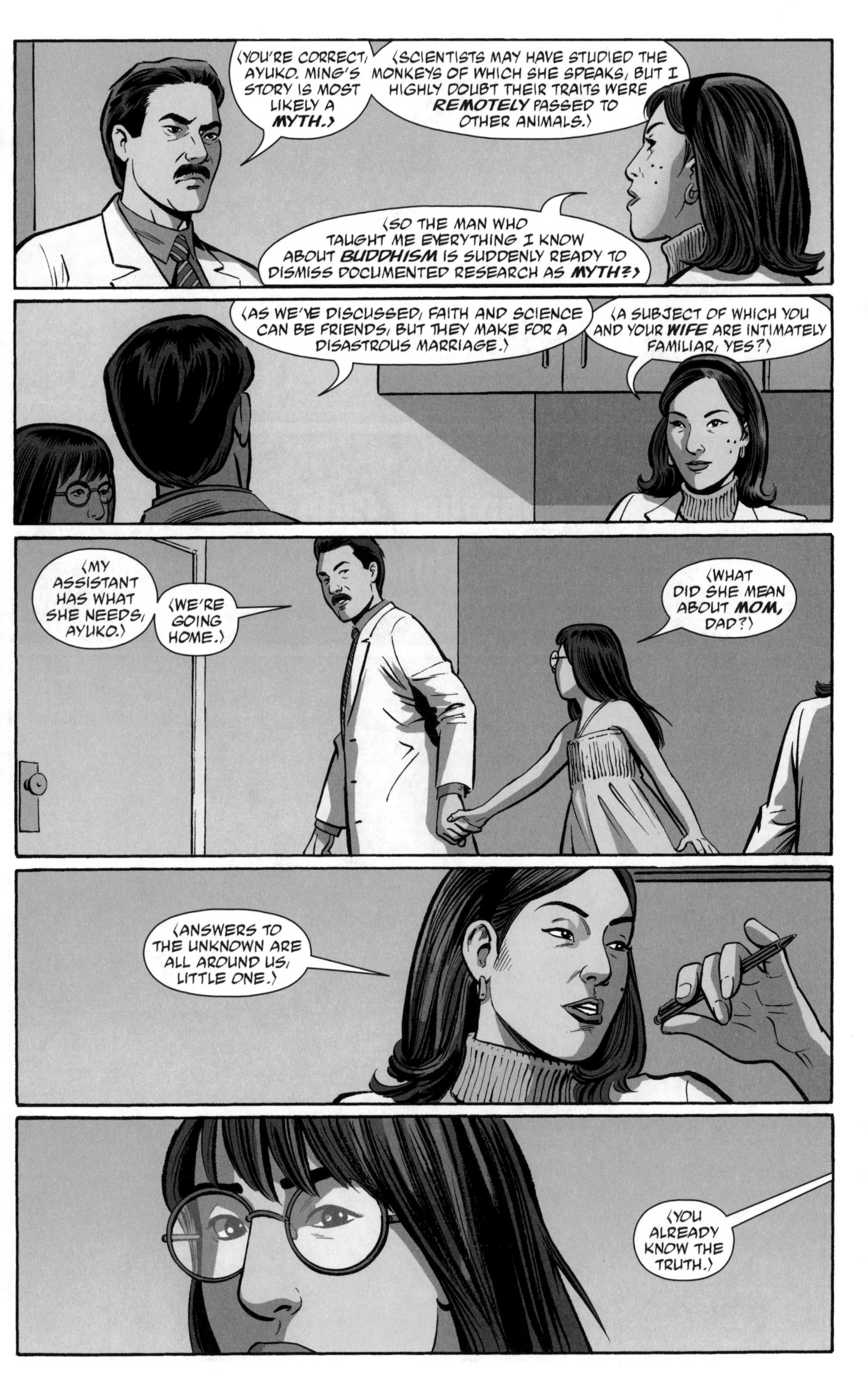

〈YOU'RE CORRECT, AYUKO. MING'S STORY IS MOST LIKELY A MYTH.〉
〈SCIENTISTS MAY HAVE STUDIED THE MONKEYS OF WHICH SHE SPEAKS, BUT I HIGHLY DOUBT THEIR TRAITS WERE REMOTELY PASSED TO OTHER ANIMALS.〉
〈SO THE MAN WHO TAUGHT ME EVERYTHING I KNOW ABOUT BUDDHISM IS SUDDENLY READY TO DISMISS DOCUMENTED RESEARCH AS MYTH?〉
〈AS WE'VE DISCUSSED, FAITH AND SCIENCE CAN BE FRIENDS, BUT THEY MAKE FOR A DISASTROUS MARRIAGE.〉
〈A SUBJECT OF WHICH YOU AND YOUR WIFE ARE INTIMATELY FAMILIAR, YES?〉
〈MY ASSISTANT HAS WHAT SHE NEEDS, AYUKO.〉
〈WE'RE GOING HOME.〉
〈WHAT DID SHE MEAN ABOUT MOM, DAD?〉
〈ANSWERS TO THE UNKNOWN ARE ALL AROUND US, LITTLE ONE.〉
〈YOU ALREADY KNOW THE TRUTH.〉

Shenzhen, China
Now

I DON'T CARE IF SHE'S SINGING A FUCKING OPERA, YORICK.
IF ROSE HURT SO MUCH AS DR. MANN'S FEELINGS, SHE STILL GETS A BULLET.
THEN KILL ME ALREADY! JUST GET ALLISON TO A BLOODY HOSPITAL!

TO FIX WHAT YOU DID?
I DIDN'T DO ANYTHING, 355! SHE'S SICK OR SOMETHING!
WHY SHOULD I BELIEVE ANYTHING YOU SAY WHEN YOU'VE DONE NOTHING BUT LIE TO US FOR THE PAST YEAR?

LIE?
MY CAPTAIN ASKED ME TO SPY ON YOUR LOT, BUT ONLY UNTIL I WAS SURE THAT THE LAST MAN ON EARTH WAS IN GOOD HANDS.
I KNOW HE IS NOW, SO I WENT OUT INTO THE COLD, DEFECTED, WHATEVER YOU WANT TO CALL IT. I SWORE MY ALLEGIANCE TO YOU. TO ALI. I LOVE HER. I--

XIANZAI... MA MA...

WHAT DID SHE SAY?
SOMETHING ABOUT HER MOTHER, I THINK.
I DON'T SPEAK CHINESE, BUT "MAMA" IS A FALSE COGNATE, MEANS THE SAME THING IN ENGLISH, SWAHILI, NAVAJO--
KEEP TALKING AND I SHOOT YOU, TOO, 'RICK.
MOM'S IN HONG KONG...WITH MING...
MING? AS IN, "THE MERCILESS"? WHAT IS SHE, HAVING ONE OF MY DREAMS?
ALI SAID MING'S A WOMAN AT SOME BIOETHICS INSTITUTE. THINKS THIS GIRL MIGHT KNOW WHAT KILLED ALL THE MEN.
WHATEVER, IF MANN'S MOTHER IS THERE, THAT'S WHERE WE'RE GOING. SHE SAVED YOUR WORTHLESS LIFE, MAYBE SHE CAN SAVE HER DAUGHTER, TOO.
OSS
I GUESS SO, BUDDY.
WE'RE OFF TO SEE THE WIZARD.

⟨ADMIRAL TSE'ELON?⟩

⟨IT'S STILL **LIEUTENANT-GENERAL,** PRIVATE.⟩
⟨I STOLE A BATTLESHIP, I DIDN'T JOIN THE FUCKING NAVY.⟩
⟨I'M SORRY, MA'AM.⟩

⟨I DON'T WANT YOUR APOLOGY, I WANT YOU TO TELL ME WE'VE INTERCEPTED THE BOAT THAT YORICK'S SISTER AND THE **CHILDREN** BOARDED.⟩
⟨NOT YET, BUT THE GIRLS IN THE RADAR ROOM SAY THAT WE SHOULD BE ABLE TO CATCH THEM BEFORE THEY REACH FRANCE.⟩
⟨THEN WHAT ARE YOU DOING IN MY QUARTERS **NOW?**⟩

⟨THIS PICTURE, LIEUTENANT-GENERAL. OF THE OTHER ARMIES **FIGHTING** OVER THE LAST MAN?⟩
⟨IT'S JUST, BEFORE I WAS DRAFTED INTO THE I.D.F., I INTERNED IN **HA'ARETZ,** AND...WELL, I'M PRETTY SURE THIS PHOTOGRAPH WAS **DOCTORED.** IT'S NOT REAL, MA'AM.⟩

⟨ELIANA, ISN'T THAT EXACTLY WHAT THE PETTY CONSPIRACY THEORISTS SAID ABOUT THE PHOTO OF **YORICK BROWN**?⟩
⟨AND HAVEN'T I **PROVED** TO YOU THAT **HE'S** ABSOLUTELY REAL?⟩
⟨YES, BUT... WITH RESPECT, MOST OF THESE GIRLS DIDN'T JOIN YOUR MISSION TO CHASE SOME MAN. THEY DID IT TO HELP BRING PEACE TO--⟩

HKK

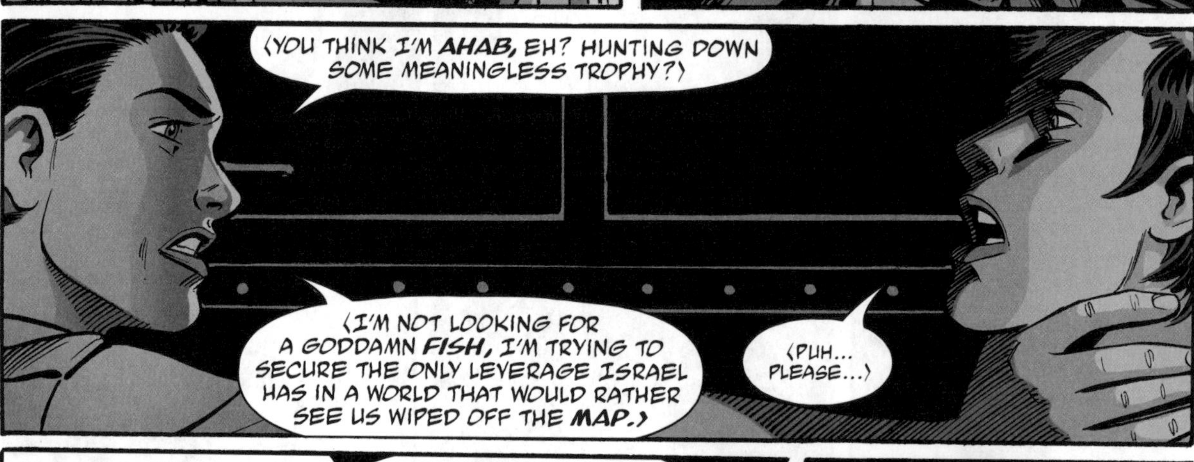
⟨YOU THINK I'M **AHAB**, EH? HUNTING DOWN SOME MEANINGLESS TROPHY?⟩
⟨I'M NOT LOOKING FOR A GODDAMN **FISH**, I'M TRYING TO SECURE THE ONLY LEVERAGE ISRAEL HAS IN A WORLD THAT WOULD RATHER SEE US WIPED OFF THE **MAP**.⟩
⟨PUH... PLEASE...⟩

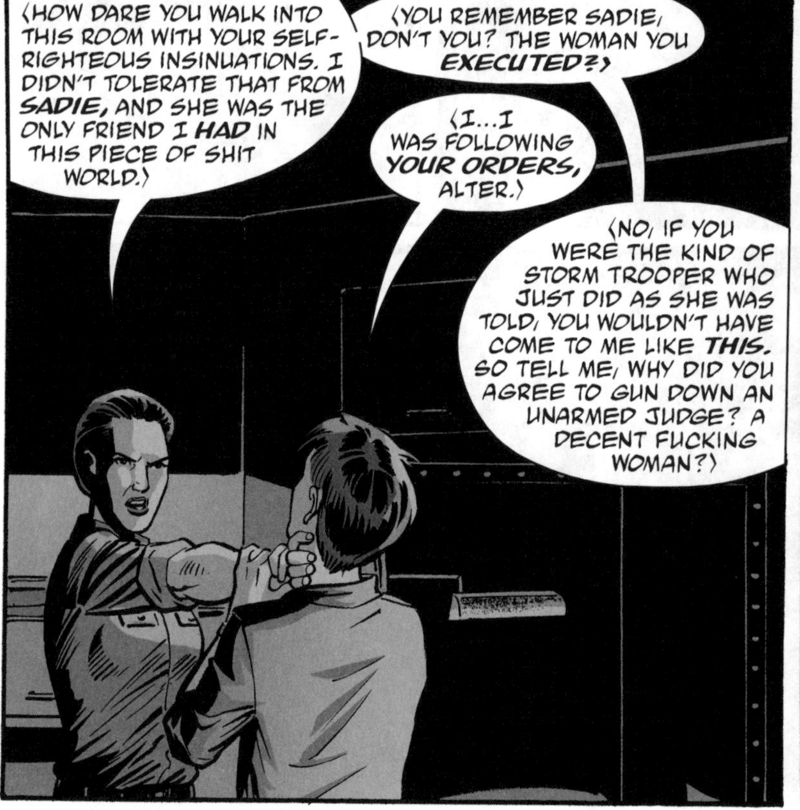
⟨HOW DARE YOU WALK INTO THIS ROOM WITH YOUR SELF-RIGHTEOUS INSINUATIONS. I DIDN'T TOLERATE THAT FROM **SADIE**, AND SHE WAS THE ONLY FRIEND I **HAD** IN THIS PIECE OF SHIT WORLD.⟩
⟨YOU REMEMBER SADIE, DON'T YOU? THE WOMAN YOU **EXECUTED**?⟩
⟨I...I WAS FOLLOWING **YOUR ORDERS**, ALTER.⟩
⟨NO, IF YOU WERE THE KIND OF STORM TROOPER WHO JUST DID AS SHE WAS TOLD, YOU WOULDN'T HAVE COME TO ME LIKE **THIS**. SO TELL ME, WHY DID YOU AGREE TO GUN DOWN AN UNARMED JUDGE? A DECENT FUCKING WOMAN?⟩

⟨**WHY DID YOU DO THAT?**⟩

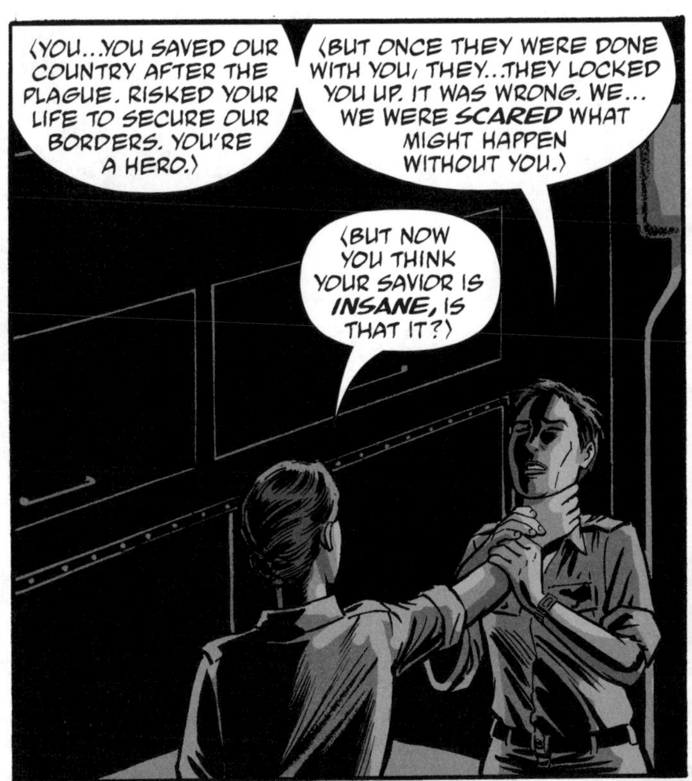
⟨YOU...YOU SAVED OUR COUNTRY AFTER THE PLAGUE. RISKED YOUR LIFE TO SECURE OUR BORDERS. YOU'RE A HERO.⟩
⟨BUT ONCE THEY WERE DONE WITH YOU, THEY...THEY LOCKED YOU UP. IT WAS WRONG. WE... WE WERE **SCARED** WHAT MIGHT HAPPEN WITHOUT YOU.⟩
⟨BUT NOW YOU THINK YOUR SAVIOR IS **INSANE,** IS THAT IT?⟩

⟨NO, YOU'RE... YOU'RE NOT INSANE.⟩

⟨THEN WHY THE HELL AM I LETTING YOU LIVE?⟩

⟨PUT THIS BACK IN YOUR LITTLE SCRAPBOOK UNTIL YOU'RE READY TO FILL MY BOOTS.⟩
⟨GO ON, OFF TO YOUR BUNK.⟩

⟨UNTIL YOU'RE READY TO DO WHATEVER IT TAKES TO DRAG GIRLS TO WAR.⟩

〈SORRY, SADIE...〉
〈...NOT TODAY.〉

HNNNNNNK
120

JUST SO YOU KNOW, YOU'RE GONNA HAVE TO CLEAN ANY DEAD RICKSHAW DRIVERS OFF OUR GRILLE ***YOURSELF.***

I KNEW I SHOULD HAVE LEFT YOU AT HOME.
WHY, SO MISTRESS STABS-A-LOT COULD SHANGHAI ME AND KIDNAP AMPERSAND AGAIN?
HFT
I REALIZE I'M IN NO POSITION TO BE ASKING QUESTIONS HERE--

GOOD, THEN SHUT UP.

IF I WENT TO ALL THE TROUBLE OF CARJACKING AN AMBULANCE, WHY NOT JUST TAKE DR. MANN TO WHATEVER *HOSPITAL* IT WAS HEADED TO?
*BECAUSE,* NO ORDINARY SURGEON IS GOING TO BE ABLE TO HELP US. IF ALLISON REALLY IS *SICK,* IT PROBABLY HAS SOMETHING TO DO WITH HER TRYING TO GIVE BIRTH TO A *CLONE* OF HERSELF.

*HERSELF?* I THOUGHT SHE WANTED TO PHOTOCOPY SOME *MALE* RELATIVE OF HERS? SO HE COULD BE HIS OWN BONE-MARROW DONOR OR WHATEVER.
THAT'S JUST A STORY SHE MADE UP TO SOUND SELFLESS. SHE WAS ACTUALLY RACING TO CLONE *HERSELF* BEFORE HER FATHER COULD CLONE *HIMSELF.*

I HAVE NO IDEA WHAT YOU PEOPLE EVER SAW IN SOAP OPERAS.
HOLD ON!

WE'RE HERE.

I WANT EVERYONE BEHIND ME.
YORICK, YOU AND ROSE WHEEL THE DOCTOR'S GURNEY INTO--
EEEE

EEEEEEEEE
RELAX, AMP.
I TOLD YOU, THERE ARE NO MONKEY-EATING BIRDS IN CHINA. MANN JUST SAID THAT AFTER YOU MASTURBATED INTO HER BAG OF--

OW!
VSSST
I JUST GOT STUNG BY SOME... KIND...OF...

YORICK!!

YOU SET US UP?!
THIS ISN'T ME! I SWEAR TO--

VSSST
VSSSST

FUCK THAT.
I'M NOT...GOING... DOWN...
NUH.

(OH, DR. M IS GONNA LOVE THIS.)

KRAK

AYUKO?

⟨CAN YOU HEAR ME?⟩

AHH!
⟨CALM YOURSELF.⟩
⟨IT'S YOUR MOTHER.⟩

⟨I KNOW WHO YOU ARE, BUT HOW THE HELL DID I GET **HERE?**⟩
⟨WHERE ARE MY **FRIENDS?**⟩
⟨TOYOTA IS DEALING WITH THE GIRLS AND THEIR ANIMALS. BUT THE DRUGS SHE USED TO INCAPACITATE THEM HAD A GREATER IMPACT ON **YORICK** THAN YOUR LADY FRIENDS...⟩

⟨...SO MY **CAPTOR** ORDERED ME TO BRING HIM HERE FOR OBSERVATION.⟩
DOC! YOU'RE **OKAY!** BUT...WHO'S THE CRAZY WITCH DOCTOR?
WHATEVER, YOU HAVE TO GET ME A **BIC PEN!** I CAN JIMMY MY WAY OUT OF THESE RESTRAINTS, BUT I--

⟨IS HE **DELIRIOUS?** IF HE NEEDS BLOOD, WE'RE BOTH **B** POSITIVE. AND YORICK'S ALLERGIC TO PENICILLIN AND SHELLFISH, SO DON'T--⟩
⟨YOUR PATIENT WILL BE **FINE,** AYUKO.⟩
⟨ALL **YOU** NEED TO WORRY ABOUT IS RECOVERING FROM SURGERY.⟩

⟨RECOVERING FROM **WHAT** SURGERY?⟩

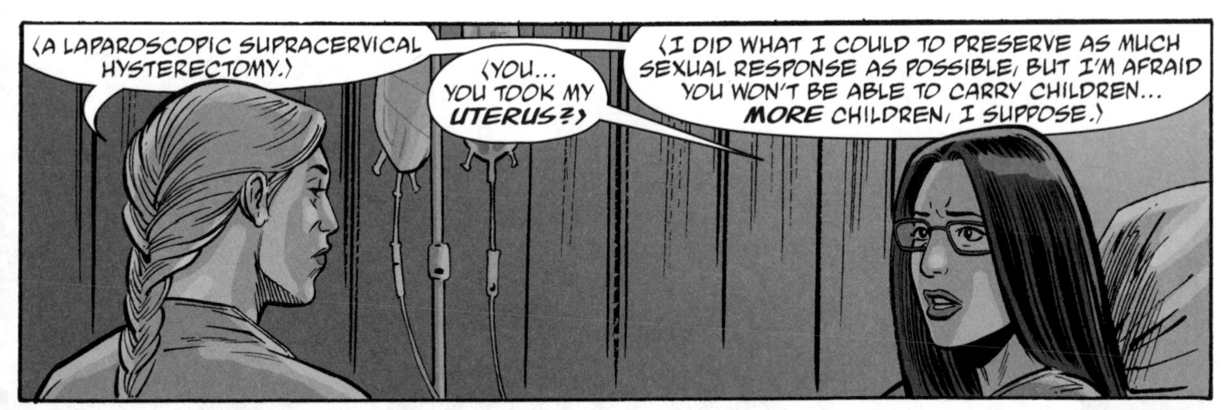
<A LAPAROSCOPIC SUPRACERVICAL HYSTERECTOMY.>
<YOU... YOU TOOK MY UTERUS?>
<I DID WHAT I COULD TO PRESERVE AS MUCH SEXUAL RESPONSE AS POSSIBLE, BUT I'M AFRAID YOU WON'T BE ABLE TO CARRY CHILDREN... MORE CHILDREN, I SUPPOSE.>

<HOW DID YOU...?>
<YOUR SYMPTOMS WERE IDENTICAL TO DR. MING'S. APPARENTLY, GENETICALLY ENGINEERED FETUSES CONTRIBUTE TO THE DEVELOPMENT OF FIBROID-LIKE TUMORS WITHIN THE WOMB.>
<THANKFULLY, YOU'RE YOUNGER AND STRONGER THAN MING WAS WHEN SHE MADE HER MISTAKE. PRIDEFUL BITCH WAS NEARLY FIFTY WHEN SHE WAS IMPREGNATED.>
UM, ANY CHANCE I COULD GET A QUICK TRANSLATION HERE?

<SHE BROUGHT A HUMAN CLONE TO TERM?>
<AND TOYOTA BROUGHT ME HERE TO SAVE HER LIFE, AFTER MING DEVELOPED COMPLICATIONS LIKE YOURS.>
<BUT THE DOCTOR WAS TOO FAR GONE. SHE DIED SHORTLY AFTER I ARRIVED.>

<IF MING IS DEAD, THEN WHO THE HELL IS THAT NINJA WHORE WORKING FOR?>
HELLO, AYUKO.

IT'S GOOD TO SEE YOU AGAIN.

OH, MAN.
NOT ANOTHER FUCKING ROBOT.

I'M TRULY SORRY FOR THIS. FOR ALL OF THE PAST FOUR YEARS.
⟨DON'T DO THIS TO HER.⟩
⟨IF YOU TELL HER EVERYTHING AT ONCE LIKE YOU TOLD ME, SHE'LL HAVE A--⟩

⟨I'LL SPEAK TO OUR DAUGHTER AS I PLEASE.⟩

BACK UP, IS THIS...?
I MEAN, IS HE REALLY...?
HOW ARE YOU STILL ALIVE, DAD?

THE SAME WAY THAT MR. BROWN IS, THOUGH THIS ISN'T ABOUT HIM OR HIS ANIMAL.
IT'S ABOUT THE PEOPLE RESPONSIBLE FOR THE PLAGUE...NAMELY ME AND MY OFFSPRING.

WHAT OFFSPRING?
ME... OR THE CLONE OF YOURSELF YOU SHOVED IN MING'S BELLY?
WHO SAID I EVER TRIED TO CLONE MYSELF?

AYUKO NI, COME HERE, PLEASE.
THERE'S SOMEONE I'D LIKE YOU TO MEET.

OHAYO.

JESUS CHRIST, IS SHE...?
YOU AT FOUR YEARS OLD? YES, AND YOU WERE EXACTLY THIS BEAUTIFUL AT HER AGE.
FROM EARLY ON, I KNEW I HAD FAILED YOU AS A FATHER, AYUKO. I'D FAILED YOU AS A MAN...

...BUT I NEVER STOPPED TRYING.

Yokogata, Japan
Fifteen Years Ago

⟨EXACTLY WHAT I WAS ABOUT TO ASK YOU. WHO SENT YOU TO BREAK INTO MY LABORATORY?⟩
⟨NOBODY, ALL RIGHT? I... I WAS JUST LOOKING FOR DOWNERS AND SHIT.⟩
⟨AND WHERE ARE YOUR PARENTS?⟩

⟨FLOATING AROUND HOKKAIDO, I GUESS.⟩
⟨THEY'VE BEEN SUCKING SALTWATER SINCE '83.⟩

⟨THE TSUNAMI? BUT, HOW DID YOU SURVIVE?⟩
⟨WHO THE FUCK KNOWS?⟩
⟨IT'S EITHER YOUR TIME TO GO OR IT ISN'T.⟩

⟨DO YOU KNOW WHO TOMOE GOZEN IS?⟩

⟨SOMEONE WHO WILL BORE THE CRAP OUT OF ME?⟩
⟨SHE WAS A FEMALE SAMURAI IN THE TIME OF THE GENPEI WAR, A LOYAL ATTENDANT TO A GENERAL NAMED YOSHINAKA.⟩
⟨TOMOE GOZEN MASTERED ARCHERY AND KETJUTSU SO THAT SHE COULD ACCOMPANY HER MASTER INTO BATTLE.⟩

⟨HOW WOULD **YOU** LIKE TO STUDY THE SAME SKILLS?⟩
⟨I'M NOT BIG INTO THE WHOLE CLASSROOM THING, THANKS.⟩
⟨THIS IS NO ORDINARY SCHOOL. I LEARNED OF IT FROM MY **ASSISTANT.** IT'S A PROGRAM THAT WILL TEACH YOU HOW TO DEFEND YOUR LIFE AND THE LIFE OF YOUR EMPLOYER.⟩

⟨I'M FIFTEEN. WHO'S GONNA EMPLOY **ME?**⟩
⟨**I** WILL. MY WORK HAS ALREADY FORCED ME OUT OF ONE COUNTRY, AND JAPAN WILL NOT WELCOME ME MUCH LONGER.⟩
⟨ONE DAY SOON, I WILL REQUIRE A COMPETENT SECURITY AGENT TO ESCORT ME PAST THOSE MEN AND WOMEN SMALL-MINDED ENOUGH TO VIEW MY RESEARCH AS **DANGEROUS.**⟩

⟨YEAH, SURE, I'LL BE YOUR BITCH.⟩
⟨FOR **ONE MILLION YEN.**⟩

⟨WHAT IS YOUR **NAME,** LITTLE THIEF?⟩

Hong Kong, China
Now

I TRAINED WITH AN ORGANIZATION CALLED THE PERFECT CIRCLE. HIROHITO FOUNDED IT BACK IN THE 1940s AS A COUNTERMEASURE TO YOUR SECRET CLUB.
BUT I ONLY SPENT A FEW YEARS AT THEIR LAME DOJO BEFORE I SOLD OUT AND WENT ALL CORPORATE.

WHAT LITTLE CODE NUMBER DID YOUR KEEPERS ASSIGN YOU AGAIN?
I'D BE HAPPY TO CARVE IT INTO YOUR BELLY SO THEY'LL BE ABLE TO IDENTIFY YOUR HEADLESS CORPSE.
NO.

IF YOU'RE GONNA KILL US BOTH, DO ME FIRST.
SHUT UP, ROSE.
IT'S ALL RIGHT, AGENT 355. I MARCHED US INTO THIS SWAMP, AND IT'LL GO FASTER FOR YOU IF WE LET HER SHARPEN THOSE KNIVES ON MY WORTHLESS BONES FIRST.

I LIVE TO SERVE.

THIS IS BULLSHIT.

WATCH YOUR LANGUAGE, AYUKO.
THEY MAY SHARE YOUR IDENTICAL NATURE, BUT YOUR "SISTERS" STILL NEED OUR NURTURE.

HOLY CRAP.
IT'S DR. MEN.

BE SILENT, YORICK.
MY HUSBAND IS A VERY SICK MAN. HE--
⟨THAT'S ENOUGH.⟩

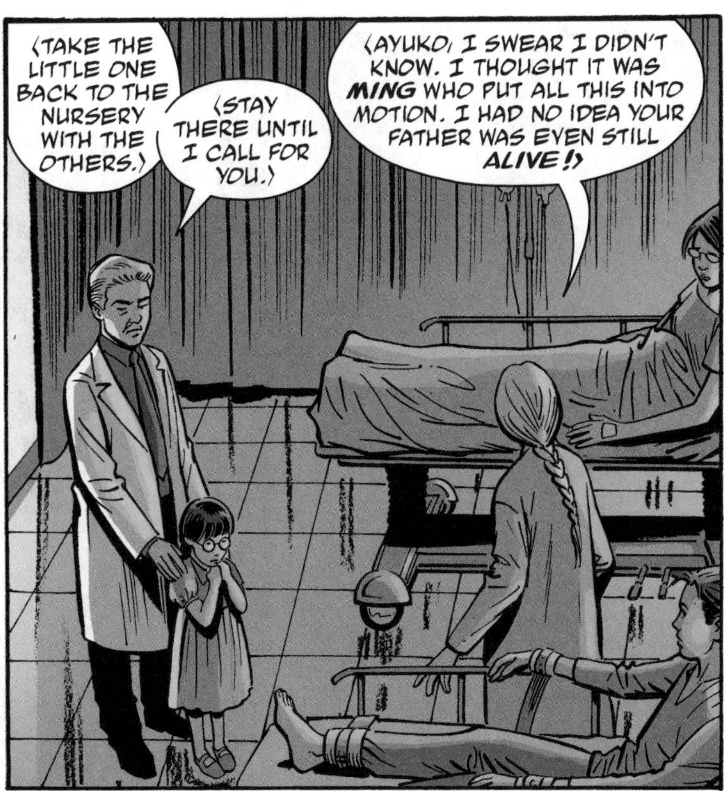
⟨TAKE THE LITTLE ONE BACK TO THE NURSERY WITH THE OTHERS.⟩
⟨STAY THERE UNTIL I CALL FOR YOU.⟩
⟨AYUKO, I SWEAR I DIDN'T KNOW. I THOUGHT IT WAS **MING** WHO PUT ALL THIS INTO MOTION. I HAD NO IDEA YOUR FATHER WAS EVEN STILL **ALIVE!**⟩

**⟨GO.⟩**
⟨YOU'VE INTERFERED WITH MY RELATIONSHIPS LONG ENOUGH.⟩

I DON'T KNOW WHAT THE **FUCK** IS HAPPENING, BUT IF YOU DON'T TELL ME WHERE MY FRIENDS ARE, I'M GOING TO BUST OUT OF THESE RESTRAINTS AND KICK YOUR MUSTACHIOED **ASS.**

RIGHT AFTER I FIND MY STUPID **PEN...**

HOW THE HELL DOES HE GET OUT OF THESE THINGS SO FAST?
I KNOW WHAT YOU'RE THINKING, AUSSIE.

"IF THAT CUNT HADN'T BLOW-DARTED ME FULL OF DRUGS, I'D TOTALLY KICK HER IN THE KIDNEYS NOW."
TOO BAD YOU'RE NOT NEARLY TOUGH ENOUGH TO GIVE IT A GO, HUH?

SPTOO

I CANNOT WAIT TO FEED YOU YOUR ONE GOOD EYE.
STOP IT. PLEASE.

I AM SO GODDAMN TIRED OF KILLING PEOPLE.
HEY, LOOKS LIKE SOMEBODY LEARNED A FEW TRICKS FROM MAGIC FAG!
DID THE WHITE BOY ALSO TEACH YOU HOW TO TAKE DOWN A YOUNGER, SEXIER OPPONENT? 'CAUSE THE ONLY HARDWARE I SEE YOU PACKING IS THOSE SAGGY TITS.
YEAH, WELL, IT'S EVERY WOMAN'S WORST ENEMY.
GRAVITY.

THE HELL WAS THAT?

I'M SURE TOYOTA WILL LOOK INTO IT.
THAT BITCH WORKS FOR *YOU?*
I THOUGHT SHE WAS ONE OF YOUR *MISTRESSES'* GOONS.

I KNEW YOUR MOTHER WOULD BE SUSPICIOUS OF ME TAKING ANOTHER YOUNG FEMALE INTO MY EMPLOY, SO I *SUBCONTRACTED* HER TO THE LATE DR. MING.
WHO GIVES A SHIT *WHO'S* SIGNING HER CHECKS?
I'M NOT GOING TO LOSE MY MONKEY TO THAT SOCIOPATH AGAIN.

"AMPERSAND," AS YOU CALL HIM, IS NOT YOURS, MR. BROWN.
THE MONKEY BELONGS TO *ME.* I RAISED THE ANIMAL FROM BIRTH.

UM, IS THAT SOME KIND OF ZEN *METAPHOR...* BECAUSE IT MAKES NO FUCKING SENSE.

WHEN JAPAN CRIMINALIZED HUMAN CLONING IN 2000, I WAS FORCED TO LEAVE MY WIFE AND MOVE HERE TO CHINA, WHERE SUCH LAWS WERE...LESS WELL DEFINED.
WITH FUNDING FROM DR. MING'S INSTITUTE, I BEGAN WORKING TO CREATE THE FIRST VIABLE HUMAN CLONE FROM THE SAMPLES OF **YOUR** GENETIC MATERIAL I TOOK YEARS PRIOR, AYUKO. I DREAMED OF HAVING A SECOND CHANCE TO RAISE YOU **HONORABLY.**

DESPITE HER AGE, MING OFFERED TO CARRY THE CLONE I DESIGNED TO TERM.
THERE WERE YOUNGER CANDIDATES--CANDIDATES WHOM WE WOULD END UP IMPREGNATING WITH **LATER MODELS** OF YOUR CLONED EMBRYOS--BUT AT THE TIME, DISCRETION TOOK PRECEDENCE OVER VIGOR.

DURING MY RESEARCH, I DISCOVERED A UNIQUE CHEMICAL COMPOUND THAT SEEMED TO HAVE AN ADVERSE EFFECT ON THE GENOMES OF CLONED MAMMALS.
WHEN I RECEIVED WORD THAT A "DR. MANN" WAS RACING TO COMPLETE HER **OWN** GENETIC DOUBLE, I KNEW I HAD TO USE THIS SERUM TO **SABOTAGE** YOUR WORK.

THAT WAS **YOU?** I...I WAS SURE IT WAS ALL **MY** FAULT.
YOU STARTED YOUR WHOLE PROJECT TO "HONOR" ME, BUT AS SOON AS YOU FOUND OUT I WAS YOUR COMPETITION, YOU DECIDED TO MURDER MY **BABY?**

I HAVE NO EXPLANATION BEYOND MY OWN SHAMEFUL PRIDE.
I BEGAN LOOKING FOR METHODS TO HALT YOUR IMPRESSIVE PROGRESS, METHODS THAT EVEN A MIND SUCH AS YOUR OWN WOULD BE UNABLE TO TRACE BACK TO ME.

KNOWING THAT YOU RELIED ON **CAPUCHINS** FOR YOUR RESEARCH, I INJECTED ONE WITH MY FORMULA AND HAD IT SHIPPED TO THE LAB WHERE YOU RECRUITED YOUR SAMPLES.
IT WAS MY HOPE THAT THE MONKEY WOULD ACT AS A **VECTOR,** LIKE THE CATS THAT TRANSFER **TOXOPLASMOSIS** TO PREGNANT WOMEN.

BUT AS I WOULD LATER LEARN, AMPERSAND WAS INSTEAD GUIDED TO **MR. BROWN** BY THE HAND OF FATE.
EITHER THAT, OR A MEANINGLESS **SHIPPING MISTAKE.**
YVR
YVR
YVR

JESUS, CAN YOU SLOW DOWN A BIT? I WASN'T THIS LOST READING HERETICS OF DUNE.
IF AMPERSAND DIDN'T END UP WITH ME UNTIL **AFTER** I LOST MY CHILD, HOW DID SHE **DIE?** AND WHAT DOES ANY OF THIS HAVE TO DO WITH WHATEVER CAUSED THE **PLAGUE?**
IT'S AS BOTH SCIENCE **AND** THE BUDDHA TEACH, AYUKO. EVERYTHING IS **ONE...**

HNF.

YOU DROPPED SOME- THING.

LET'S HOPE YOU'RE AS LOUSY WITH A **NAGINATA** AS I REMEMBER YOU BEING WITH A KATANA.
IF YOU'D RATHER RUN YOUR MOUTH THAN FIGHT, THAT'S FINE BY ME.

COOL.
LET'S TALK ABOUT THE FACT THAT YOUR MOM WAS PROBABLY A BIG FAT **WHORE.**

KLACK
KLACK
UHN!

SHANG

NAH!

TOYOTA WAS MY FAIL-SAFE.
WHEN MY FIRST PLAN APPEARED UNSUCCESSFUL, I SENT HER TO THE STATES TO POISON YOUR UNBORN CHILD IN A MORE CONVENTIONAL MANNER.
MING WAS DAYS AWAY FROM GIVING BIRTH, AND THOUGH YOU WERE WEEKS BEHIND OUR EFFORTS, I COULDN'T RISK YOUR REACHING EVEN PREMATURE DELIVERY BEFORE US.
SO I HAD TOYOTA, WHO'S BEEN GOOD ENOUGH TO SHADOW YOU EVER SINCE, LACE ONE OF YOUR MEALS WITH AN ABORTIFACIENT TO TERMINATE YOUR PREGNANCY.
HOURS LATER, MING'S CONTRACTIONS BEGAN IN THIS VERY ROOM. LABOR WAS SURPRISINGLY EASY, BUT WHAT CAME NEXT WAS NOT.
THE SECOND MY CLONE OF YOU TOOK HER FIRST BREATH, THE GLOBAL MISERY FOR WHICH I AM RESPONSIBLE BEGAN.

DAD, THE TIMING COULD BE A...A COINCIDENCE. IT DOESN'T PROVE THAT YOU CAUSED THE PLAGUE.
THE GENDERCIDE MAY HAVE APPEARED INSTANTANEOUS, BUT BY ALL ACCOUNTS OF THE DEATHS THAT FOLLOWED, THE "SHOCK WAVE" SPREAD JUST SHY OF THAT, AT 186,000 MILES PER SECOND.
BY MY CALCULATIONS, THAT MAKES THESE VERY COORDINATES GROUND ZERO FOR THE PLAGUE.

HOW CAN A DISEASE TRAVEL AT THE SPEED OF LIGHT?
AND WHY DIDN'T IT KILL THE ASTRONAUT GUYS?

ALL LIFE IN THE UNIVERSE MAY NOT BE CONNECTED... BUT ALL LIFE ON OUR PLANET IS.
MING'S RESEARCH CONVINCED ME THAT WE ARE SURROUNDED BY THE BIOLOGICAL EQUIVALENT OF ELECTROMAGNETIC FIELDS.
MORPHO-GENETICS? YOU ALWAYS TOLD ME THAT WAS A MYTH!

AND A FEW YEARS AGO, I WOULD HAVE SAID THE SAME ABOUT HUMAN CLONING.

ONE DAY, A GROUP OF CHIMPANZEES LEARNS TO SMASH OPEN NUTS WITH A STONE HAMMER, AND ACROSS A RIVER, THOUSANDS OF MILES AWAY, OTHER CHIMPS SUDDENLY KNOW HOW TO USE THE SAME TOOL.
ONE DAY, A SINGLE MAN UNLOCKS THE SECRET OF ASEXUAL HUMAN REPRODUCTION, AND ACROSS THE PLANET, MEN ARE INSTANTLY RENDERED EXTINCT.
THERE IS NO DENYING THAT EVOLUTION IS A PROCESS IN WHICH WE ARE ALL ACTIVELY INVOLVED. IT'S SURVIVAL OF THE FITTEST, AND SOMETHING OUT THERE DECIDED THAT MALES WERE NO LONGER FIT TO SURVIVE.

SO IF YOUR IMMACULATE CONCEPTION KILLED ALL THE MEN, THEN THE STUFF YOU INJECTED AMP WITH TO PREVENT SOMEBODY ELSE'S VIRGIN BIRTH HAD THE OPPOSITE EFFECT?
IT SHIELDED THE TWO OF US FROM, WHAT...GOD'S WRATH?

NO, THERE'S NO FUCKING "INTELLIGENT DESIGNER."
THERE HAS TO BE A **RATIONAL EXPLANATION** FOR WHY THE Y CHROMOSOME WOULD SUDDENLY SELF-DESTRUCT.

THE Y CHROMOSOME HAS BEEN RATIONALLY SELF-DESTRUCTING FOR HUNDREDS OF MILLIONS OF YEARS.
IT USED TO CONTAIN THOUSANDS OF WORKING GENES, BUT WAS WHITTLED DOWN TO JUST A FEW DOZEN EVEN **BEFORE** THE PLAGUE.

MEN HAVE LONG BEEN A NECESSARY EVIL FOR THE CONTINUATION OF THIS SPECIES, BUT THE MOMENT THAT EVIL BECAME ***OBSOLETE,*** NATURE RIGHTED ITS COURSE.
I WAS MERELY THE ***TRIGGER*** THAT SET OFF A TIME BOMB THAT'S BEEN TICKING FOR MILLENNIA.
DEET DEET
***MNN...***

WHAT DID YOU ***DO*** TO HER, DR. MOREAU?
IT'S ONLY A MORPHINE DRIP, YORICK. SHE IS STILL RECOVERING FROM SURGERY, AND NEEDS HER SLEEP.
BESIDES, I THOUGHT IT WAS TIME YOU AND I TALK ALONE.
MAN TO MAN.

WHY ARE YOU DOING THIS?

BECAUSE MY BOSS SAYS YOU'RE DANGEROUS.
HE PROBABLY WOULD HAVE LET YOU LIVE IF YOU'D JUST MINDED YOUR OWN BUSINESS.

"HE"?

DR. M IS MANN'S FATHER.
AND NO MATTER WHAT THAT UNGRATEFUL DYKE TOLD YOU, HE'S AN ALL RIGHT GUY.

HE'S GONNA HELP ME LIVE FOREVER.
KRACK

YOU'RE...AN IDIOT.

THAT'S WHAT I TOLD DR. M, BUT THEN HE SHOWED ME ALL THE TEST-TUBE BRATS HE ENGINEERED. SAYS HE'S ONLY GONNA MAKE COPIES OF CERTAIN GIRLS, AND I'M ONE OF THEM.
A THOUSAND YEARS FROM NOW, THERE WILL STILL BE A WHOLE LINE OF WOMEN EXACTLY LIKE ME WALKING THE PLANET. I'LL NEVER REALLY DIE.

THEN I DON'T FEEL SO BAD ABOUT WHAT HAPPENS NEXT.

KINDA DREW THE SHORT END OF THAT STICK, HUH?

YEAH.

BUT SOMETIMES, THAT'S...

...ENOUGH.

I'M NOT AN EVIL MAN.

YOU KNOW WHAT KIND OF PEOPLE HAVE TO SAY THAT, RIGHT?
I'VE DONE TERRIBLE THINGS IN MY LIFE, BUT THIS... THIS WAS AN ACCIDENT.
I VOWED TO FIND YOUR PET AND DO WHATEVER I COULD TO BRING MANKIND BACK TO THE PLANET.

AND YET, OVER THE LAST FOUR YEARS, I'VE WATCHED THE WOMEN OF THIS COUNTRY MAKE SUCH REMARKABLE PROGRESS WITHOUT US.
IS IT LIKE THAT ALL OVER THE WORLD?
I DON'T KNOW. I GUESS SO. WHATEVER, I JUST WANT TO FIND MY GIRLFRIEND. HER NAME IS BETH. SHE--

DR. MING, THE WOMAN I LOVED, DIED IN MY ARMS JUST A FEW DAYS AFTER MY WIFE ARRIVED. IT REMINDED ME WHAT CRUEL CREATURES MEN ARE.
OUR BODIES TELL US TO LOVE SO MANY, BUT THERE'S ROOM IN OUR HEARTS FOR SO FEW. WE'RE IMPOSSIBLY FLAWED ANIMALS, AREN'T WE?

ANYWAY, AYUKO CAN CONTINUE MY WORK. SHE AND HER MOTHER WILL SEE THAT WOMEN LIVE ON BEYOND THIS GENERATION.
BUT YOU AND I... WE DIDN'T BELONG IN THIS WORLD BEFORE THE PLAGUE, AND WE CERTAINLY DON'T BELONG HERE NOW.

IT'S TIME FOR US TO GO.

I GUESS THIS IS GOODBYE.

Saint-Nazaire, France
Now

WHAT IN HELL ARE YOU TALKING LIKE THAT FOR, HERO?
LOOK, NATALYA, THE ENTIRE ISRAELI DEFENSE FORCES ARE PROBABLY STILL ON OUR ASSES, AND THERE'S NO GUARANTEE WE'LL FIND YORICK BEFORE THEY FIND ME AND BETH.
YEAH, JUNIOR HERE NEEDS TO MEET HER FATHER, BUT YOU AND CIBA SHOULD PRESS ON TO MOSCOW. GET BABY VLAD AS FAR AWAY FROM DANGER AS POSSIBLE.

NO CHANCES. IF I LEAVE YOU TWO AND A HALF HELPLESS GIRLS BY LONESOME, YIDDISH WOMENS WILL KILL YOU ALL.
BESIDE, KREMLIN IS TOO HARSH FOR MAN-CHILDREN AT THIS TIME OF YEAR, EVEN FOR SON OF **COSMONAUT.**

I HAVE NO IDEA WHAT SHE JUST SAID, BUT I KNOW I WOULDN'T LAST AN **HOUR** WITH NAT AS MY ONLY CONVERSATION PARTNER.
HER ENGLISH ISN'T BROKEN, IT'S **ANNIHILATED.**
<A MILLION TIMES BETTER THAN YOUR **RUSSIAN,** SWEETHEART.>

I'M SORRY, I HATE TO BREAK UP THE YA-YA SISTERHOOD--
HEY, THAT WAS THE LAST MOVIE I SAW RIGHT BEFORE THE PLAGUE HIT. I WONDER IF **IT** KILLED ALL THE MEN ON IMPACT? DEATH BY CHICK FLICK.
--BUT THIS IS **SERIOUS.** OUR LITTLE CAT AND MOUSE GAME IS ONLY GOING TO GET MORE DANGEROUS ONCE WE'RE LANDLOCKED. ASSUMING YORICK AND HIS **OTHER** BETH ARE EVEN HERE YET, I CAN'T GUARANTEE WE'LL ALL, YOU KNOW, SURVIVE THE REUNION.

THANKS, HERO, BUT WE'RE NOT **ABANDONING** YOU GUYS.
I DON'T WANT A LIFE FOR VLADIMIR WITHOUT YOUR **BROTHER** IN IT. I KNOW IT'S OLD-FASHIONED...

...BUT I REALLY THINK BOYS NEED A STRONG MALE INFLUENCE.

**Hong Kong, China**
**Now**

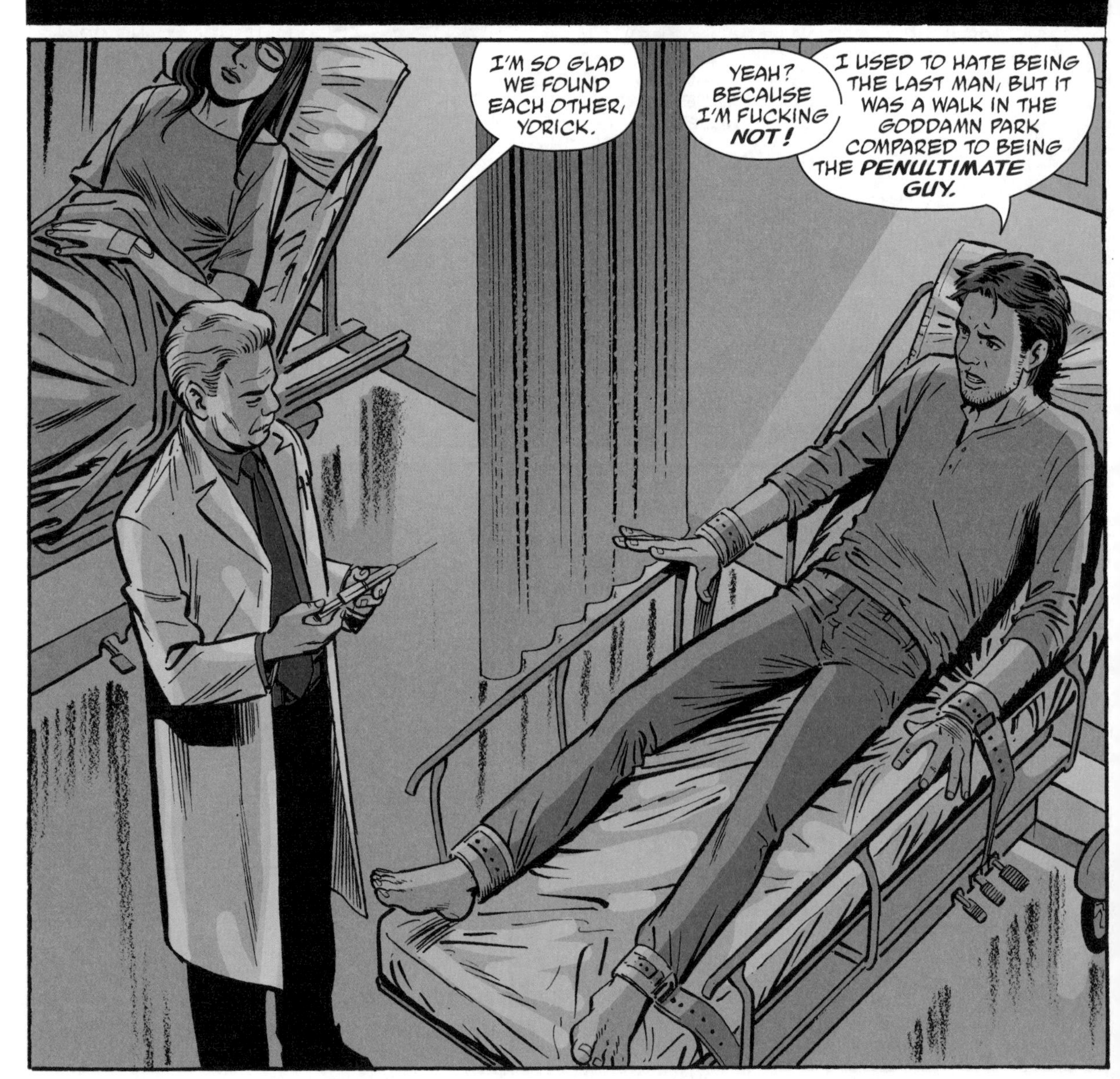

EVER SINCE I WAS A LITTLE BOY, WOMEN HAVE TERRIFIED ME. I SUSPECT THIS IS WHY MY MALE COLLEAGUES AND I **MARGINALIZED** SO MANY LATER IN LIFE.
OUR SEXES MAY BE EQUAL, BUT THEY ARE NOT THE SAME.

I'D HOPED WE COULD ALL FIND A WAY TO COEXIST, BUT EVOLUTION CLEARLY PREFERS THE IDEA OF **SEGREGATION,** A NEWLY PASSED NATURAL LAW BY WHICH YOU AND I MUST ABIDE.
LOOK, A FEW YEARS AGO, I WOULD HAVE BEEN TOTALLY DOWN WITH YOUR SUICIDE PACT, ACE.
I MADE UP ALL SORTS OF EXCUSES ABOUT HOW **OFFING MYSELF** AND LEAVING THIS WORLD TO THE LADIES WOULD BE NOBLE AND SELFLESS AND--

I'M SORRY, BUT THIS GRAND EXPERIMENT ISN'T OPEN TO PEER REVIEW.
JUST SHUT UP AND LISTEN TO ME, MATSUMORI! EVERY GUY GOES THROUGH A PERIOD WHERE HE'S...HE'S SCARED SHITLESS AND COMPLETELY BAFFLED BY GIRLS, RIGHT?
BUT THEN WE'RE SUPPOSED TO **GROW UP,** FIGURE OUT THAT THE BEST PLACE FOR ALL THE GREAT WOMEN PROBABLY ISN'T **BEHIND** EVERY GREAT MAN.

THE TWO SIDES ARE ONLY GONNA GET THROUGH THIS TOGETHER...SO WHY DON'T YOU STOP BEING SUCH A **PUSSY** AND MAN THE **FUCK** UP?

IF WE BELONGED IN THIS WORLD, THE GENDERCIDE NEVER WOULD HAVE HAPPENED.
OH, SELL THAT "IF MAN WERE MEANT TO FLY" BULLSHIT TO SOMEBODY ELSE.
MAYBE GOD OR BUDDHA OR XENU OR WHOEVER DIDN'T GIVE US WINGS, BUT HE DID GIVE US ENOUGH GRAY MATTER TO BUILD DC-10S, RIGHT?

SO YEAH, MAYBE THERE IS A REASON HE OR SHE OR IT WIPED OUT EVERY OTHER PENIS ON THE PLANET, BUT THAT MEANS THERE'S ALSO A REASON THE TWO OF US GOT LEFT BEHIND!
YOU SHOULD FEEL VERY LITTLE PAIN, YORICK.
THERE ARE ENOUGH BARBITURATES IN HERE TO FELL A MAN TWICE YOUR SIZE.

WHERE'S THAT GUY WHEN YOU NEED HIM?

JUST...JUST PROMISE NOT TO HURT DR. MANN AFTER YOU DO ME.
MY DAUGHTER WILL BE PERFECTLY ALL RIGHT, YORICK. I TOLD YOU, I ONLY GAVE HER A SEDATIVE.
NO, YOU DIDN'T.

YOU JUST THOUGHT YOU DID, DAD.
I UNHOOKED MY MORPHINE DRIP THE SECOND YOU WALKED INTO THE ROOM.

YOU NEVER DID PAY ENOUGH ATTENTION TO ME.

HELP!
CAN ANYBODY HEAR ME?
EVERY-ONE CAN.

PLEASE, YOU'RE FRIGHTENING THE CHILDREN DOWNSTAIRS. I APOLOGIZE FOR OUR CURRENT SITUATION, BUT I IMPLORE YOU TO BE QUIET.
YOU'RE ALLISON MANN'S MUM, RIGHT? SHE'S GOT YOUR NOSE.
AND YOU'RE HER... HER...
GIRLFRIEND, YEAH. IS THAT WHY YOU'VE CHAINED ME UP HERE? 'CAUSE YOU'RE A BLOODY HOMOPHOBE?

I AM GRATEFUL IF MY DAUGHTER HAS FOUND ANYONE TO LOVE IN THIS WORLD. AND I AM AS MUCH A PRISONER IN THIS PLACE AS YOU.
WHICH IS WHY YOU MUST REMAIN SILENT. THE LAST TIME I TRIED TO SUMMON ASSISTANCE, TOYOTA NEARLY CUT OFF MY HANDS.
YOU MEAN THAT NINJITSU BIRD?

SHE AND 355 KIND OF STEPPED OUTSIDE.

DEAR GOD.
ARE THEY...?
WHAT DO YOU THINK I WAS GOING ON ABOUT? I'VE BEEN YELLING AT THE TOP OF MY LUNGS, BUT NEITHER OF THEM HAS SAID A WORD BACK!

AIYAH.
UM, MY CHINESE IS A LITTLE RUSTY, MA'AM. DOES THAT MEAN AGENT 355'S OKAY OR NOT?
THAT DEPENDS.

HAVE YOU EVER ASSISTED IN A SURGERY BEFORE?

I DON'T WANT TO HURT YOU.
BUT, AS ALWAYS, IF I MUST...

IT'S IMPORTANT THAT YORICK AND I END THIS ALONE, AYUKO.
STOP CALLING ME THAT. MY NAME IS DOCTOR ALLISON MANN, AND YOUR HOSTAGE IS MY PATIENT.
DOC, DON'T! GET OUT OF HERE BEFORE--

OVER THE LAST FOUR YEARS, I HAVE CLEANED HIS WOUNDS AND EMPTIED HIS BEDPANS, SET HIS BROKEN BONES AND CURED HIM OF A DOZEN DIFFERENT KINDS OF FOOD POISONING.
I HAVE INVESTED WAY TOO MUCH OF MY MEDICAL GENIUS ON HIS PIMPLED ASS TO LOSE HIM ON THE TABLE NOW.

YOU'VE JUST HAD YOUR WOMB CARVED OUT. YOU'RE IN NO CONDITION TO FIGHT ME.
JUST LET ME FINISH WHAT I STARTED.

GO AHEAD.
BUT KNOW THAT I WILL SPEND THE REST OF MY NATURAL LIFE WORKING TO BRING MEN, EVEN ASSHOLES LIKE YOU, BACK TO THIS PLANET.

NO, YOU WON'T.
AND WHY THE HELL NOT?

BECAUSE THE FIRST CLONED GIRL KILLED ALL THE MEN.
WHAT MAKES YOU THINK THE FIRST CLONED BOY WON'T KILL ALL THE WOMEN?

NO.

NO, FUCK THAT! A GIRL DIDN'T DESTROY MAN-KIND, YOU DID. YOU WERE RECKLESS AND...AND SLOPPY AND YOU LET YOUR EGO GET IN THE WAY OF YOUR SCIENCE.
AND HOW ARE YOU ANY DIFFERENT?
BECAUSE I LEARN FROM MY MISTAKES. I CARE ABOUT PEOPLE OTHER THAN MYSELF, AND I OWE IT TO THEM TO GET THIS RIGHT. I WILL GET IT RIGHT.
YOU KNOW, CUTTING YOUR UMBILICAL WAS THE LAST TIME I WAS EVER TRULY HAPPY.

I DON'T KNOW WHY.
UHN!

BASTARD!

IT'S FUNNY, ISN'T IT?
THE ENGLISH WORD FOR **MERCY KILLING** IS--
OTO-SAN?

⟨I HEARD NOISES.⟩

AYUKO!
⟨GET BACK TO THE NURSERY! RIGHT--⟩

NAAH!

AH.

AND SO...

AIEEEE!

⟨I'M... I'M SORRY, AYUKO.⟩

⟨I'M SO SORRY.⟩

Shenzhen, China
Two Weeks Later

ALLISON. AM I...?
BACK AT THE SAFEHOUSE.
MOM WAS CONCERNED YOU WEREN'T HEALING FAST ENOUGH IN DAD'S HERMETICALLY SEALED WONDERLAND, SO SHE ORDERED ME TO GET YOU SOME FRESH AIR.

I USED TO THINK HER HOMEOPATHIC SHTICK WAS NONSENSE, BUT THIS IS THE SECOND TIME SHE'S PULLED ONE OF MY FRIENDS BACK FROM THE BRINK.
OUCH.
I GUESS ROSE AND I MATCH NOW, HUH?

NOT EXACTLY. TOYOTA DID SOME REAL DAMAGE THIS TIME, THREE-FIFTY.
SHE ANGLED HER BLADE IN SUCH A WAY THAT IT SEVERED BOTH OF YOUR FALLOPIAN TUBES. WE REPAIRED WHAT WE COULD...

...BUT I'M AFRAID MOTHERHOOD WILL NEVER BE AN OPTION.

SERIOUSLY? OH, THANK CHRIST.
I...I THOUGHT YOU WERE GOING TO TELL ME I WAS PARALYZED OR SOMETHING. I MEAN, IT'S NOT LIKE ANYONE'S AROUND TO GET ME PREGNANT.

UNLESS... YOU WEREN'T EXPECTING ME TO CARRY ONE OF YOUR CLONED BOYS, WERE YOU?
NO, ROSE HAS SELFLESSLY VOLUNTEERED FOR THAT LINE OF DUTY.
SHE'S AWARE OF THE POSSIBLE COMPLICATIONS, BUT SHE HAS FAITH IN MY WORK.

YEAH, WELL, I'M SORRY I DIDN'T HAVE FAITH IN HER.
ROSE RISKED HER LIFE TO HELP ME BACK IN HONG KONG, ALLISON. SHE'S A GOOD WOMAN.
WELL, SHE'S GOOD FOR ME.

BUT, IF YOU'RE NOT LOOKING FOR A BIRTHING SURROGATE, WHO DID YOU THINK I'D EVER MAKE BABIES WITH?
THREE-FIFTY, I RECOGNIZED IT THE SECOND YOU TWO FIRST SET FOOT IN MY LAB WAY BACK IN BOSTON.
IT'S TIME TO ADMIT THAT YOU'RE IN LOVE WITH YORICK.

...THE FUCK?

WE'VE BEEN OVER THIS. I KNOW I MUTTERED SOMETHING TO THAT EFFECT THE LAST TIME I WAS IN ONE OF YOUR SICKBEDS, BUT THAT WAS JUST--
--BECAUSE YOU CONFUSED YOUR PROTECTIVE INSTINCTS WITH ROMANTIC FEELINGS?
NO, THAT'S WHY YOU SLEPT WITH ME. BUT THERE'S SOMETHING ELSE GOING ON WITH YOU AND HIM, WHETHER YOU WANT TO ADMIT IT TO YOURSELF OR NOT.

I GET PEOPLE WHERE THEY NEED TO BE.
AND RIGHT NOW, YORICK NEEDS TO BE WITH HIS GIRLFRIEND.

IF YOU SAY SO.
I JUST HOPE YOU FIND TIME TO GET YOURSELF WHERE YOU NEED TO BE.

IDIGI LIDIGOVE YIDIGOU.

IDIGI LIDIGOVE YIDIGOU, TIDIGOO.

WAIT, YOU'RE GOING TO BE MY MOM?
WELL, ALI AND HER MUM ARE GOING TO DO THEIR BEST TO KNOCK ME UP WITH YOUR GENETIC DUPLICATE, YEAH.
AND SINCE BONNY'S OFFSPRING IS SUPPOSEDLY GOING TO HAVE THE SAME MAGICAL FECES AS AMPERSAND, I THINK WE STAND A DECENT CHANCE OF MAKING ALL THIS STICK, ASSUMING MY GIRL CAN ISOLATE THE SHITE THAT SAVES BOYS FROM THE SHITE THAT KILLS CLONES.
WOW, MY MOTHER IS GOING TO BE A SMOKING HOT LESBIAN. IT'S A FREUDIAN NIGHTMARE.
ANYWAY, TRY TO BE PATIENT WITH HIM, OKAY?
YOUR SON'S GOING TO BE A NAIVE, SELF-RIGHTEOUS DOUCHE FOR THE FIRST FEW YEARS, BUT HE SHOULD BE COMPLETELY AWESOME BY THE TIME HE'S, LIKE, FORTY-FIVE.
I'LL KEEP THAT IN MIND, LAST MATE.
SHE'S AWAKE, ROSE.
THREE-FIFTY WANTED TO SAY GOODBYE TO YOU BEFORE WE LEAVE.

CHEERS, LOVE.
SAY SO LONG TO YOUR BOYFRIEND, BONNY.
FEA

YOU GUYS ARE HEADED BACK ALREADY? BUT SLEEPING BEAUTY JUST WOKE UP!
I KNOW, BUT MY MOTHER IS MANNING THE NURSERY ALL BY HER LONESOME, AND SHE COULD BARELY HANDLE ONE OF ME.
ANYWAY, YOU AND AGENT 355 CAN CATCH THE TRANS-SIBERIAN TO PARIS FROM HERE AS SOON AS SHE'S FEELING UP TO THE TRIP.

SHE'S RECOVERING NICELY, BUT I CAN'T GUARANTEE SHE'LL EVER BE BACK TO HER FULL FIGHTING STRENGTH, SO STAY OUT OF TROUBLE FOR ONCE, WILL YOU?
DOC, THERE'S...THERE'S NO WAY I CAN THANK YOU FOR WHAT YOU DID BACK IN H.K. FOR EVERYTHING YOU'VE DONE FOR ME.
SO INSTEAD, I'M JUST GONNA BE A DICK AND ASK FOR ONE LAST FAVOR.

IN ALL THE YEARS WE'VE BEEN PLAYING HARD-TRAVELING HEROES, I DON'T THINK I'VE SEEN YOU SMILE ONCE.
WHAT'S A GUY HAVE TO DO TO CHANGE THAT?

AHUHH

AHUHHUHUH
OH. OH, CRAP.
JESUS, DOC, I WOULD HAVE SETTLED FOR A LOPSIDED GRIN. A SARCASTIC SMIRK?

THE TIME I HAVE SPENT WITH YOU AND YOUR STUPID MONKEY HAS BEEN AMONG THE UNHAPPIEST OF MY LIFE.

I HAVE NO IDEA WHY I'M GOING TO MISS YOU SO MUCH.

LISTEN TO ME.
YOU HAVE A BIG HEART...
UGH, STOP! THIS HAS BEEN SAPPY ENOUGH. I WANT TO REMEMBER YOU BELITTLING MY MANY SHORT-COMINGS, NOT LEAVING ME WITH A COMPLIMENT.

ENLARGED HEARTS ARE WEAK AND FRAGILE, YORICK.
IT WASN'T A COMPLIMENT, IT WAS A WARNING.

WHATEVER HAPPENS IN FRANCE, YOU...YOU JUST STAY STRONG, OKAY?
YEAH YEAH, AN APPLE A DAY.
GOOD LUCK SAVING THE WORLD, ALLISON.

SAME TO YOU, MR. BROWN.

PARDONNEZ-MOI.

AVEZ-VOUS VU CET HOMME?

S'IL VOUS PLAIT.

CAFE
DAGUERRE
AVEZ-VOUS VU CET HOMME?

Arlington, Virginia
Months Ago

BACK UP, YOU *PRETEND* TO BE PART OF THE PATRIARCHY?
IF YOU LET ME LIVE, I'LL...I'LL MAKE LOVE TO YOU BOTH.
EVERYBODY TELLS ME MY EQUIPMENT FEELS REAL. *ALMOST.* AND I'VE BEEN WORKING ON MY UPPER BODY, SO I CAN HOLD YOU JUST AS TIGHT AS ANY--

HOW DARE YOU HONOR THE *PEDERASTS* MOTHER EARTH SAW FIT TO *DESTROY?*
PLEASE.
I JUST CAME HERE TO SEE WHERE MY *DAD* WAS BURIED. I... I NEVER EVEN HAD A CHANCE TO MEET HIM.

WE CAN FIX THAT.
BLAM

I CAN'T LEAVE YOU LITTLE BITCHES ALONE FOR A *SECOND,* CAN I?

STEP OFF BEFORE I SLAP YOU BOTH.
SHE'S A MAN WHORE, BOSS!
I DON'T CARE IF SHE'S OSAMA BIN FUCKING LADEN, I DIDN'T HIRE YOU TO TERRORIZE VISITORS.
NOW EITHER GET TO WORK OR GO BACK TO EATING OUT OF THE D.C. LANDFILLS.

YOU OKAY, LADY?
YOU'RE...YOU'RE VICTORIA, AREN'T YOU?
THE AMAZONS' LEADER?

HARDLY. DAUGHTERS OF THE AMAZON KILLED MY LAST BOYFRIEND, POST-OP FEMALE-TO-MALE TRANSSEXUAL.
ARE YOU...?
NAH, JUST A CROSSDRESSER.

TOO BAD. ANYWAY, I WAS PRETTY PISSED AT THE ONE-TITTED WONDERS, BUT I REALIZED MOST OF THEM ARE JUST SCARED CHICKS LOOKING FOR THREE HOTS AND A COT.
SO I STARTED LURING THEM AWAY FROM A LIFE OF BLOWING UP MONUMENTS AND BURNING DOWN SPERM BANKS WITH THE PROMISE OF AN ACTUAL CAREER.

STILL, YOU CAN TAKE THE GIRL OUT OF THE AMAZONS, BUT YOU CAN'T ALWAYS TAKE THE AMAZONS OUT OF THE GIRL, RIGHT?
SORRY IF THEY SCARED YOU, MISS...?
BOBBI. YOU CAN CALL ME BOBBI.

COOL, I'M WAVERLY.
HOW ABOUT YOU, BOB? LOOKING FOR A STEADY GIG?

ABSOLUTELY.
I CAME ALL THE WAY FROM MISSOURI TO FIND MYSELF A PIMP AS GOOD AS YOU.

HA, I DON'T KNOW IF I SHOULD BE INSULTED OR...NO, I SHOULD BE INSULTED.
SERIOUSLY? BUT, YOU SAID THOSE TWO WORK FOR YOU.
I JUST FIGURED, WITH THE "COMFORT INDUSTRY" BEING SO BIG THESE DAYS, WHENEVER THERE ARE PRETTY GALS ROAMING PUBLIC PARKS AT NIGHT...

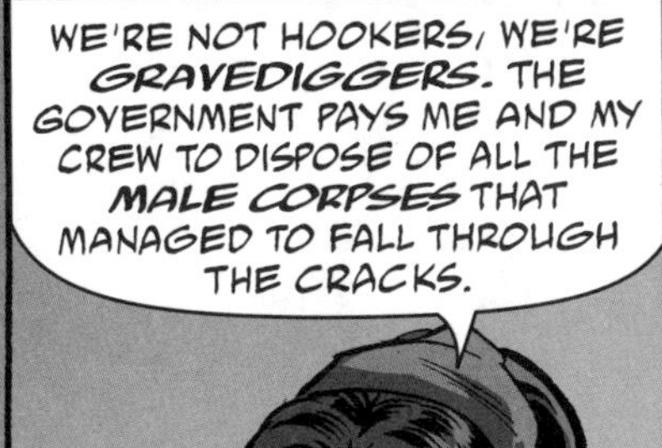
WE'RE NOT HOOKERS, WE'RE GRAVEDIGGERS. THE GOVERNMENT PAYS ME AND MY CREW TO DISPOSE OF ALL THE MALE CORPSES THAT MANAGED TO FALL THROUGH THE CRACKS.

I TAKE IT YOU WEREN'T IN THIS LINE OF WORK BEFORE THE GENDERCIDE?
NOT EVEN A LITTLE.
YEAH, 'CAUSE YOU LOOK LIKE YOU USED TO BE A MODEL.

FUCK THAT SHIT.
I WAS A SUPER-MODEL.

NICE WHEELS.
YOU SHOULD HAVE SEEN MY LAST RIDE.
IT GOT JACKED BY SOME BLACK GIRL WITH DREADS THE SAME NIGHT I RAN INTO A...

RAN INTO A WHAT?
NOTHING. BACK IN THE BAD OLD DAYS, HAULING ROTTING MAN-CARCASSES BY MYSELF ALL NIGHT USED TO MESS WITH MY HEAD.
THIS ONE TIME, I THOUGHT I HAD A CONVERSATION WITH A GUY... AND NOT A DECOMPOSED ONE, MIND YOU. BUT IT WAS PROBABLY JUST 'CAUSE I RAN OUT OF THE MEDS THIS PLASTIC SURGEON I WAS NAILING USED TO GIVE ME.

YOU'RE SURE YOU WERE HALLUCINATING?
BECAUSE THE NEWSPAPERS HAVE BEEN RUNNING THIS PICTURE OF A LIVING MALE SOMEBODY SPOTTED IN AUSTRALIA.

I DON'T READ THOSE RAGS, BOB. EVERYTHING IN 'EM IS FAKE.
TRUST ME, I'VE HAD ENOUGH LINES AIRBRUSHED OUT OF MY FAT NECK TO KNOW THAT MOST PHOTOS ARE SCIENCE FICTION, ANYWAY.

ANDELAY, HOMBRE.
I'LL SHOW YOU HOW US NINE-TO-FIVERS EARN A LIVING.
UM, IT'S AFTER MIDNIGHT, WAVERLY.

WHATEVER, GRAB MY FLASHLIGHT FROM THE GLOVE, WILL YA?
I GOT A REQUEST FROM SOME WOMAN SAYING HER HUSBAND WAS WORKING IN THE SEWERS WHEN EVERYTHING WENT DOWN. I'VE BEEN CLEARING TUNNELS ALL WEEK LOOKING FOR HIM.

WAIT, WE'RE GOING DOWN A MANHOLE?
NAH.

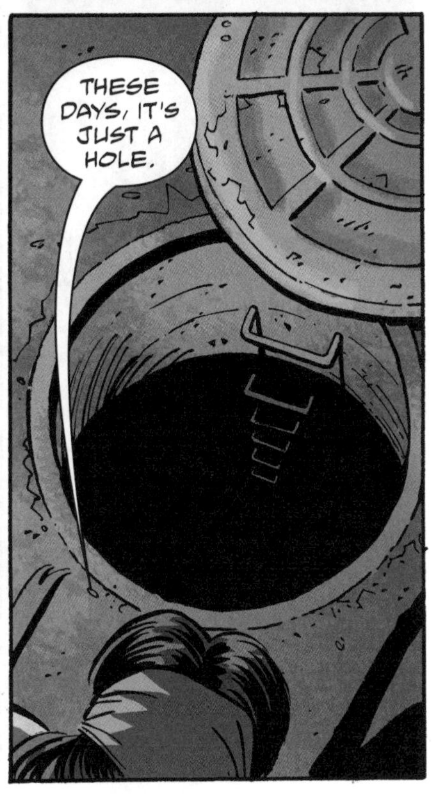
THESE DAYS, IT'S JUST A HOLE.

JUST SO YOU KNOW, THE SECOND I SEE A RAT, I'M OUT OF HERE.
WOW, HOW DID YOU EVER CONVINCE ANYONE YOU WERE A DUDE?
BESIDES, RATS ONLY LIVE THIRTY-SIX MONTHS TOPS, AND SINCE THE PLAGUE KILLED OFF EVERY MALE MAMMAL, MINNIE MOUSE RAN OUT OF THINGS TO BREED WITH YEARS AGO.

SO THEY'RE ALL GONE?
LIKE THE PIED PIPER BLEW INTO TOWN. ONLY THING YOU HAVE TO WORRY ABOUT NOW IS BUGS. THOSE STORIES ABOUT ALLIGATORS DOWN HERE ARE JUST OLD WIVES' TALES.
HOPEFULLY.

GOD, AFTER ALL THIS TIME, WHAT DOES A WOMAN STILL WANT WITH HER HUSBAND'S BONES?
"CLOSURE," I GUESS? WE DON'T PROMISE A DECENT BURIAL, BUT I CAN AT LEAST GIVE HIM A SPOT IN SECTION 60...
...AREA THEY WERE RESERVING FOR ALL THE AFGHANISTAN CASUALTIES.
REALLY? DOESN'T SEEM FAIR TO BURY HIM THERE IF HE'S NOT A VETERAN.

THEY'RE ALL VETERANS, BOBBI.
UNLUCKY LOSERS IN THE BATTLE OF THE SEXES.

WHAT ABOUT THE ANIMALS? ARE THEY JUST COLLATERAL DAMAGE?
I MEAN, THOSE AMAZONS THINK THE PLANET KILLED THE MEN, FOR EVERYTHING THEY DID TO HURT US OR WHATEVER ...BUT WHY TAKE ALL THE INNOCENT DOGS AND STUFF, TOO?

I DON'T KNOW, ASK NOAH.
CHRIST, YOU SOUND LIKE THE CRAZY CAT LADY WHO RUNS THE PET CEMETERY IN BALTIMORE.
KZZK -AVERLY, OVER? KZZK

SPEAK UP, MELINDA. I GET RECEPTION FOR ASS DOWN HERE.
YOU GOT A CALL FROM THE CAPITOL, BELIEVE IT OR NOT.
THEY FOUND A STIFF IN CONGRESS, AND THEY NEED YOU TO PICK IT UP TONIGHT, OVER.

WHAT'S THE HURRY? HE'S STILL GONNA BE DEAD IN THE MORNING, ISN'T HE?
THAT'S THE THING, BOSS. KZZK IT'S NOT A HE.

OVER.

THANK YOU FOR COMING, MA'AM. AND, ER, SIR.
MAY I INTRODUCE YOU TO THE PRESIDENT OF THE UNITED STATES, MARGARET VALENTINE.

IT'S AN HONOR TO MEET YOU, MADAME PRES--
HOLD ON, DO I KNOW YOU?
WEREN'T YOU WITH THE BROAD WHO STOLE MY GARBAGE TRUCK THE NIGHT I--

YOUNG LADY, I LOST A FRIEND TODAY. I WAS TOLD THAT YOU COULD HELP ME.
YEAH. UM, SURE. I'VE ONLY DONE A HANDFUL OF GIRLS BEFORE, BUT I CAN DOLL HER UP FOR AN OPEN CASKET IF THAT'S WHAT YOU'RE LOOKING FOR.
HOW'D SHE GO, SUICIDE OR ACCIDENTAL OVERDOSE?

SHE WAS ASSASSINATED.

CONGRESSWOMAN JENNIFER BROWN SERVED THE PREVIOUS ADMINISTRATION WITH DISTINCTION BEFORE I MADE HER MY SECRETARY OF THE INTERIOR.
YOU GUYS ALMOST LOOK LIKE *SISTERS*.
ANY CHANCE WHOEVER SHOT HER WAS ACTUALLY GUNNING FOR YOU?

***WE'LL*** BE HANDLING THE INVESTIGATION, WAVERLY.
WE'RE PAYING ***YOU*** TO TAKE CARE OF THE FUNERAL ARRANGEMENTS.

CUSTOMER'S ALWAYS RIGHT.
OKAY, FIRST UP, I'LL NEED TO GET HER OUT OF THIS GROSS ALMOST-A-PANTSUIT THING AND INTO SOMETHING WORTH SPENDING ETERNITY IN. IF EITHER OF YOU HAS...

MOTHERFUCK ME.

THIS KID.

WHO IS THIS *KID?*

THAT'S YORICK. HE WAS HER SON.
WAS? OR *IS?*
THIS ISN'T ABOUT HIM. *PLEASE.*

WE JUST WANT TO LAY HER TO REST.

Welcome
to the
Watergate

COME AGAIN?

NO ANNOYING REFRACTORY PERIOD, YOU KNOW? IT'S NOT LIKE I LOSE INTEREST AFTER THE FIRST POP.
BEST PART OF BEING A **FAKE GUY.**

THAT'S REDUNDANT, BOB.

SMOKE?
OF WHAT, A STALE MARLBORO?
OUR SIDE HAS GOTTEN IT TOGETHER ENOUGH TO START MANUFACTURING GODDAMN **MAXI PADS** AGAIN, WHEN ARE THEY GONNA ROLL SOME FRESH VIRGINIA SLIMS?

YOU'RE STILL UPSET ABOUT HER, HUH?
THAT WOMAN WHO GOT MURDERED?

I'M NOT UPSET, I'M GRATEFUL.
SHE GAVE ME SOMETHING.

HOW DO YOU MEAN?
I KNOW I SOUND MORE INSANE THAN EVER, BUT IT TOOK A DEAD WOMAN TO TELL ME MAYBE I'M NOT THE BIPOLAR LUNATIC I'VE ALWAYS THOUGHT I WAS.
AND FOR THAT, SHE DESERVES BETTER THAN ANOTHER HOLE IN THE DIRT. HER FAMILY DESERVES BETTER.

WHAT, LIKE A PRINCESS DIANA SENDOFF?
NAH, THAT ELTON JOHN SHIT WAS TACKY. I DON'T KNOW EXACTLY HOW OR WHY, BUT THIS WOMAN WAS...WAS IMPORTANT. SHE'S EARNED SOMETHING WITH CLASS.
WELL, W.W.J.D.?
CHRISTIAN CRAP DIED WITH FALWELL, THANKS.

NO.
WHAT WOULD JACKIE DO.

YEAH.

GOOD CALL.

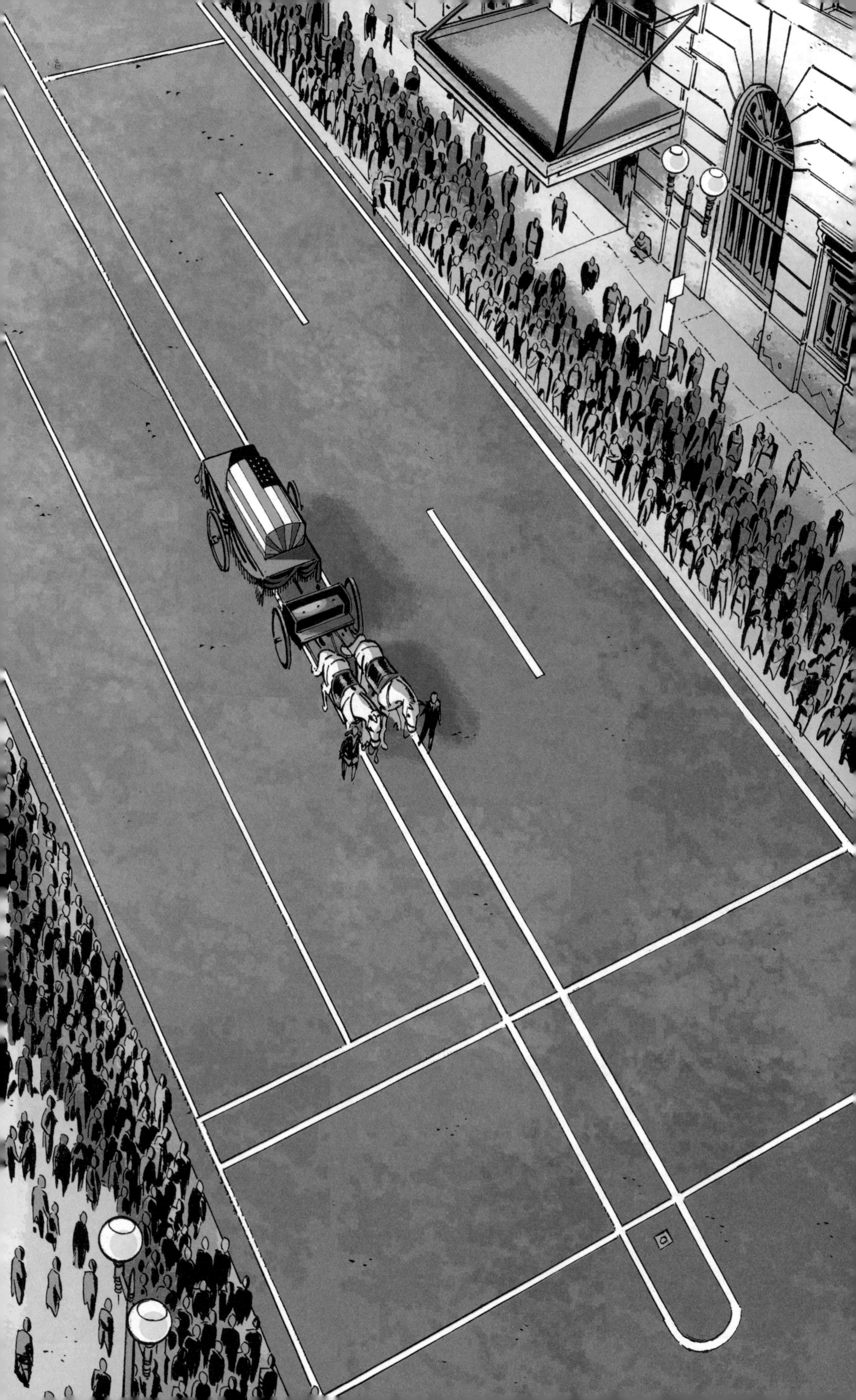

I HEARD SOME SECRET SERVICE AGENT SAY THIS WAS GONNA BE THE **FIRST TIME** A WOMAN HAS EVER LAIN IN STATE IN THE ROTUNDA.
CAN YOU BELIEVE THAT?

YEP.

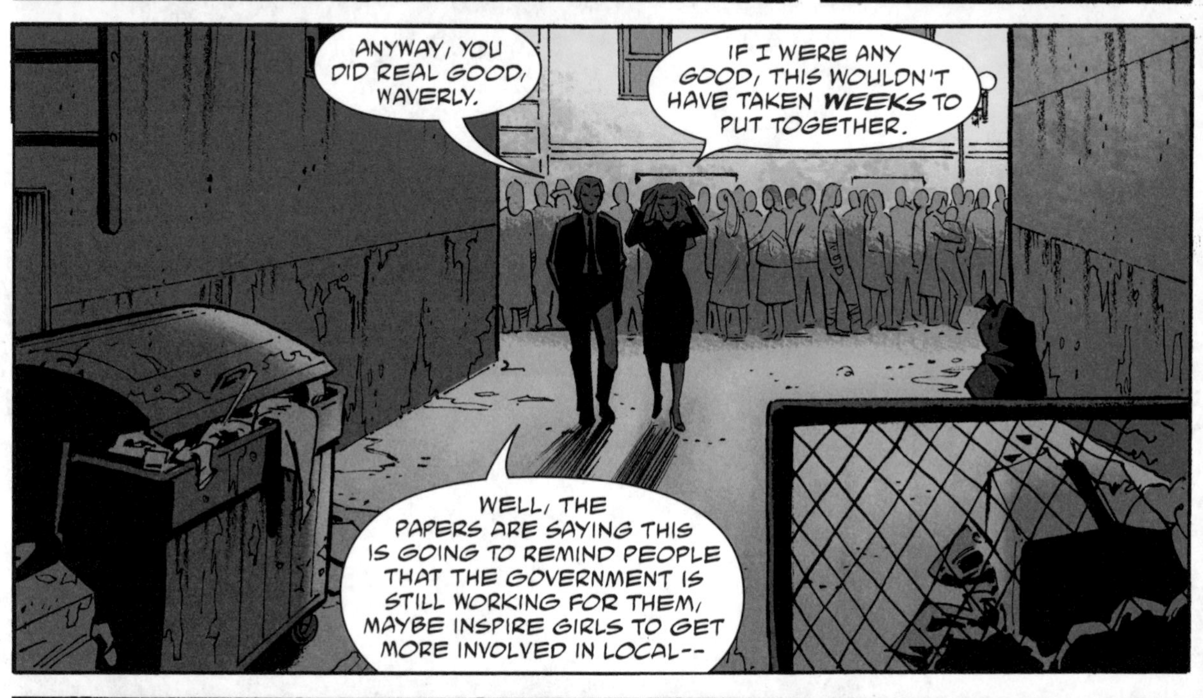
ANYWAY, YOU DID REAL GOOD, WAVERLY.
IF I WERE ANY GOOD, THIS WOULDN'T HAVE TAKEN **WEEKS** TO PUT TOGETHER.
WELL, THE PAPERS ARE SAYING THIS IS GOING TO REMIND PEOPLE THAT THE GOVERNMENT IS STILL WORKING FOR THEM, MAYBE INSPIRE GIRLS TO GET MORE INVOLVED IN LOCAL--

AHH!
JESUS, **WHAT?**

THEM.

I THOUGHT YOU SAID THE RATS ALL DIED YEARS AGO!

THEY DID. BUT THOSE ONES LOOK YOUNG.
THEN HOW...?
BECAUSE IF IT'S A MIRACLE, IT'S A PRETTY LAME ONE.

MAYBE IT'S SOME KINDA SIGN?
OF WHAT?
HELL IF I KNOW. BUT IF THE VERMIN ARE MAKING A COMEBACK, MAYBE WE'RE NOT GOING TO BE THE LAST OF OUR KIND, EITHER.
BUT WHY?

I USED TO SHOOT WITH THIS ONE FAG PHOTOGRAPHER WHO ALWAYS SAID, "ACTING MAKES IT SO."
IF YOU COME TO THE SET ALL P.M.S.-Y, JUST ACT LIKE YOU'RE THRILLED TO BE IN FRONT OF THE CAMERA, AND SOONER OR LATER, YOU WILL BE.
SO IF WE START ACTING LIKE IT'S NOT THE END OF THE WORLD ANYMORE...?

SOONER OR LATER, MAYBE IT WON'T BE.

THIS IS THE FUTURE, HUH?
IF CONGRESS WAS SERIOUS ABOUT AWARDING US THAT CONTRACT, YEAH.
BACK IN '02, THE C.D.C. USED THIS JOINT AS A MAKESHIFT CREMATORIUM, BUT NOW VALENTINE WANTS TO TURN RFK INTO A SOLAR ENERGY PLANT OR SOMETHING. ONWARD AND UPWARD.

THE OLD FIRES WERE NEVER REALLY HOT ENOUGH TO TOAST THE BOYS THROUGH AND THROUGH, SO WE'RE GONNA HAVE OUR WORK CUT OUT FOR US WITH THE CLEANUP.
ACTUALLY, THAT'S WHAT I WANTED TO TALK WITH YOU ABOUT, WAVERLY...
THESE PAST FEW MONTHS HAVE BEEN REALLY SPECIAL, BUT I'M...I'M JUST NOT BUILT TO DO WHAT YOU DO.

WHAT ARE YOU TALKING ABOUT?
YOU'RE QUITTING?
I'M GOING BACK TO MISSOURI, BACK TO THE ONLY THING I'VE EVER BEEN GOOD AT.

BULLSHIT.
WHAT ARE YOU--

RIIP
OWW!

YOU'RE BETTER THAN THAT, BOBBI. THE DAYS OF US SELLING OUR TITS AND ASS ARE OVER.
YOU'RE SMART, OKAY? WAY SMARTER THAN ME. YOU HAVE BRAINS AND...AND HEART AND AN ANNOYINGLY KIND FUCKING SPIRIT.

ME AND YOU FINALLY HAVE A SHOT TO BE MORE THAN WHATEVER EVERYONE USED TO SEE US AS.

WE CAN BE MORE THAN JUST BODIES.
THE OBITUARIST

HOLLYWOOD

# TRAGICOMIC

YOU NEVER SAID THERE WERE GONNA BE AMAZONS, MASHA!
A76-H01

I TOLD YOU THIS WAS NO REGULAR HEIST, OLGA!
WE'RE NOT KNOCKING OVER FIRST NATIONAL, WE'RE ROBBING A SPERM BANK!

WHAT'S THE POINT? THE LAST THING THIS WORLD NEEDS IS MORE GIRLS.
I MEAN, EVEN IF THIS STUFF DIDN'T SPOIL IN THE BLACKOUTS, THE PLAGUE DESTROYED ALL THE LITTLE-BOY SEMEN!
WRONG, IRINA. THE MAP I FOUND PROVES THAT THIS SAMPLE WAS SHIELDED.

WE'VE GOT THE LAST MAN-SPUNK ON EARTH.

UHN!

NO!
AHN!

DIE, YOU SONS OF BITCHES!
KLICK
KLICK
KLICK

HAND OVER THE SEED, SISTER.

GET YOUR OWN, CUM-GUZZLERS.
UHF!

AHK!

YOU'RE A TRAITOR TO YOUR SEX, SMUGGLER.
AND AS YE SOW EVIL...

...SO SHALL YE REAP.
BLAM
OWW!
I TOLD THEM TO BE MORE CAREFUL WITH THEIR FUCKING SQUIBS!
I HAVE VERY SENSITIVE NIPPLES!
CUT!

Los Angeles, California
Whenever

AND YOU SHOULDN'T HAVE TO EITHER, "SISTER." I THOUGHT OUR LITTLE VÉRITÉ PRODUCTION WAS SUPPOSED TO BE CASTING REAL AMAZONS.
I WAS A REAL DAUGHTER OF THE AMAZON, BITCH.
MAYBE, BUT YOU'RE SURE AS SHIT NOT A REAL ACTOR.

CHRIST, WILL YOU SAVE THE DRAMA FOR WHEN WE'RE ROLLING, EDIE?
VELVET MAY BE NEW TO THIS, BUT SHE DESERVES THE SAME RESPECT AS EVERYONE ELSE ON THIS SET.
IF THAT'S TRUE, THEN HOW COME ALL MY DIALOGUE IS SO LAME?

WHAT?
HERE WE GO...

YOU TOLD US THIS FLICK WAS GOING TO BE ABOUT EMPOWERING WOMEN, SO THEY WOULDN'T DECIDE TO JOIN A GANG LIKE WE DID.
BUT THIS IS NOTHING BUT ANOTHER GARBAGE ACTION MOVIE, EXACTLY WHAT THE PATRIARCHY USED TO CHURN OUT.

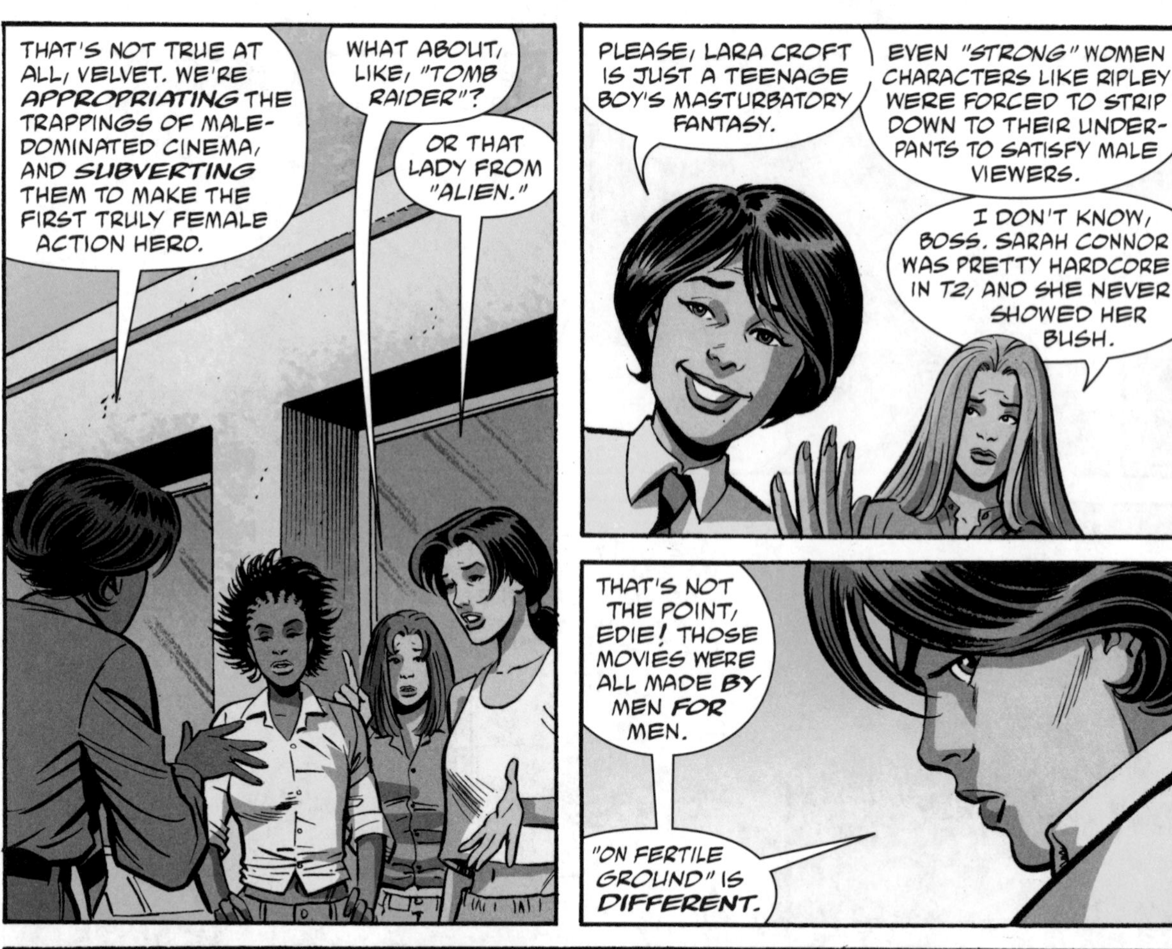
THAT'S NOT TRUE AT ALL, VELVET. WE'RE *APPROPRIATING* THE TRAPPINGS OF MALE-DOMINATED CINEMA, AND *SUBVERTING* THEM TO MAKE THE FIRST TRULY FEMALE ACTION HERO.
WHAT ABOUT, LIKE, "TOMB RAIDER"?
OR THAT LADY FROM "ALIEN."
PLEASE, LARA CROFT IS JUST A TEENAGE BOY'S MASTURBATORY FANTASY.
EVEN "*STRONG*" WOMEN CHARACTERS LIKE RIPLEY WERE FORCED TO STRIP DOWN TO THEIR UNDER-PANTS TO SATISFY MALE VIEWERS.
I DON'T KNOW, BOSS. SARAH CONNOR WAS PRETTY HARDCORE IN *T2*, AND SHE NEVER SHOWED HER BUSH.
THAT'S NOT THE POINT, EDIE! THOSE MOVIES WERE ALL MADE *BY* MEN *FOR* MEN.
"ON FERTILE GROUND" IS *DIFFERENT*.

WHATEVER, IT'S STILL *CRAP*.
COME ON, WE'RE GOING BACK TO THE GROTTO.
WAIT, YOU'RE QUITTING MY MOVIE SO YOU CAN WORK AT THE *PLAYBOY MANSION*?

IT'S A *HOSPICE*, AND SAY WHAT YOU WILL ABOUT THE BUNNIES, BUT AT LEAST THEY'RE HELPING PEOPLE.

THIS MAKE-BELIEVE NONSENSE ISN'T HELPING *JACK*.

BUT...BUT YOU SIGNED CONTRACTS!
DON'T BOTHER, LUV. OUR LAWYERS ARE ALL EPITAPHS NOW, REMEMBER?
BESIDES, WE'VE GOT ENOUGH COVERAGE TO EDIT AROUND THEM. WE CAN SHOOT THE MISSING SCENES WITH JUST STAND-INS AND EDIE.

YEAH, ABOUT THAT, HENRIETTA.
I, UH... ACTUALLY THINK THIS IS WHEN I SHOULD BOW OUT, TOO.

ARE YOU FUCKING KIDDING ME?
I'M GOING BACK TO BROADWAY, CAYCE. LOOK, I LOVED WHEN WE WERE TOURING THE COUNTRY, PUTTING ON "THE LAST MAN" FOR PACKED THEATERS. I DIDN'T SIGN UP FOR SHOOT-OUTS AND CAR CHASES.
BUT, EVEN WHEN WE WERE PLAYING TO FULL HOUSES, WE'D ONLY REACH A FEW HUNDRED WOMEN A WEEK. NOW THAT THE ELECTRICITY IS COMING BACK, WE HAVE A CHANCE TO TALK TO MILLIONS.

I GUESS, BUT I'D RATHER DO SOMETHING GREAT FOR A FEW PEOPLE THAN DUMB EVERYTHING DOWN JUST TO BE PALATABLE TO THE MASSES.
THAT'S...THAT'S NOT QUITE FAIR, EDIE.
WOW, THAT MAY BE THE LEAST CONVINCING DEFENSE I'VE EVER HEARD. FINE, IF THAT'S THE WAY EVERYBODY FEELS...

...THEN FISH & BICYCLE PICTURES IS OFFICIALLY DEAD.

WHAT DID WOODY ALLEN SAY ABOUT L.A.?
"I DON'T WANT TO MOVE TO A CITY WHERE THE ONLY CULTURAL ADVANTAGE IS BEING ABLE TO MAKE A RIGHT TURN ON A RED LIGHT."
FUCKING EXACTLY. I CAN'T BELIEVE THIS PLACE IS EVEN WORSE THAN "DAY OF THE LOCUST" MADE IT OUT TO BE.

CAREFUL, DEARIE. YOU KNOW HOW NATHANIEL WEST DIED, RIGHT?
KILLED IN A CAR ACCIDENT OVER IN EL CENTRO. SOONER OR LATER, THIS TOWN GETS ITS REVENGE ON THOSE WHO SPEAK ILL OF IT.

MAYBE THAT'S WHAT ENDED WOODY & CO.

I'M SORRY, BUT I'M SO TIRED OF MOURNING THE OLD GUARD.
YOU KNOW HOW MANY WOMEN GOT NOMINATED FOR A BEST DIRECTING OSCAR IN ALL THE DECADES BEFORE THE PLAGUE HIT? FUCKING TWO.
NEVER MIND THE FACT THAT THE AWARD ITSELF WAS NAMED AFTER A DUDE.
LISTEN, WE GAVE IT OUR BEST, AND WE KNEW WE'D PROBABLY GET RIDDEN HARD AND HUNG UP WET, NO?
ONWARD AND UPWARD THEN. I FOR ONE AM LOOKING FORWARD TO GETTING BACK TO MY OILS.
PAINTING? NO OFFENSE, BUT ISN'T THAT A LITTLE SELFISH?
I MEAN, ROME IS BURNING, HENRIETTA. WE HAVE A RESPONSIBILITY TO CREATE ART THAT BETTERS PEOPLE.
AND THAT'S WHERE YOU AND I HAVE ALWAYS DIFFERED, CAYCE. ART HAS NO RESPONSIBILITY EXCEPT TO BE ART. WE DON'T GET TO DECIDE WHICH WORKS CHANGE LIVES AND WHICH ONES MERELY...
JUST A MOMENT, I THOUGHT WE WERE HEADED TO THE 405. WHY IN THE WORLD DIDN'T WE TAKE THE 101?
101 STILL HAS TOO MANY FOUR-WHEELED COFFINS CLOGGING THE ONRAMPS. WHY, WHAT'S SO BAD ABOUT THIS ROUTE?
IT'S TAKING US RIGHT THROUGH THE WORST PART OF THE CITY!
BOY'S TOWN.

SINCE WHEN DID WEST HOLLYWOOD BECOME SKID ROW?
AROUND THE SAME TIME ALL THE GAY BARS TURNED INTO IMPROMPTU **MAUSOLEUMS.**
"WEHO" IS NO MAN'S LAND NOW, QUITE BLOODY LITERALLY.

WILL YOU RELAX, YOU BIG BABY?
WHAT ARE YOU AFRAID OF, **QUEER GHOSTS** ATTACKING OUR--

AHHH!
SKREEEECH

HEH, GLOBAL.

ARE YOU GIRLS ALL RIGHT?
WHAT ARE YOU DOING PLAYING IN THE MIDDLE OF THE GODDAMN--

GET AWAY FROM THE RIDE, YA OLD BAGS.

WHO ARE YOU CALLING OLD, YOU DESPICABLE LITTLE HARPY?
NICE TRY, KIDS, BUT MY PRODUCER AND I WORK WITH PROP GUNS ALL DAY.
WE KNOW WHAT A WATER PISTOL LOOKS LIKE WHEN WE--

BLAAM

JESUS!
KASHRINK

WE PAINT OUR HEATERS LIKE TOYS SO WE CAN GET THE DROP ON MARSHALS.
"HEATERS"? YOU'RE...YOU'RE CHILDREN!
I DIDN'T THINK THE AMAZONS STARTED RECRUITING GIRLS BEFORE YOU'D HAD YOUR FIRST PERIODS.

THOSE DYKES ARE YESTERDAY'S WEAK SAUCE, LADY.
FUTURE BELONGS TO THE FATHERFUCKIN' LAST GIRLS.

VRRRMMMM

ONWARD AND UPWARD.

AMELIA
EARHART

YOU KNOW, THEY SAY SHAKESPEARE MIGHT HAVE BEEN A WOMAN.
WHO'S "THEY," PRECISELY?
PROFESSORS, I GUESS.
HEARTSTRINGS

THEY THINK HIS STUFF WAS WRITTEN BY THIS COUNTESS, MARY SIDNEY, BECAUSE NO MAN COULD HAVE CAPTURED SO MANY VIVID EMOTIONAL DETAILS.

TRUTH OR BOLLOCKS?
I USED TO THINK THERE WAS A POSSIBILITY, BUT NOW I REALIZE IT'S INSANE.
WOMEN DON'T KNOW ANY-THING ABOUT LOVE OR...OR BEAUTY. WE'VE HAD THIS PLANET TO OURSELVES FOR *YEARS* NOW, AND ALL WE'VE FILLED IT WITH IS BACKSTABBING AND UGLINESS.

NOW
NOW, WHILE MOST OF THE BAD EGGS DO SEEM TO ROLL OUR WAY, I'D SAY THAT WOMANKIND HAS ACQUITTED HERSELF QUITE ADMIRABLY, SO FAR AS APOCALYPSES GO.
JUST IMAGINE HOW DREADFUL THINGS WOULD BE IF ONLY THE *LADS* HAD SURVIVED.

WHAT ARE YOU *READING*, ANYWAY?
SOMETHING ONE OF OUR GANGSTER-ETTES DROPPED.
COMIC BOOK, EVER THE ENTERTAINMENT CHOICE FOR JUVENILE DELINQUENTS.

COMICS?

OH LORD, I KNOW *THAT* LOOK.
AND MUCH AS I DISLIKE CONSTANTLY DASHING YOUR DREAMS, MIGHT I REMIND YOU THAT OUR PRODUCTION BUDGET CURRENTLY CONSISTS OF HALF A PACK OF FAGS AND THE HORRID CLOTHES ON OUR BACKS?

WE'VE ALSO GOT MY WRITING AND YOUR ART. WHAT MORE DO WE NEED?

ER, A WORKING KNOWLEDGE OF THE MEDIUM? *PAPER* MIGHT BE HELPFUL, TOO.
IT'S JUST WORDS AND PICTURES, HENRIETTA.
THIS FORMAT HAS ALL THE ADVANTAGES OF FILM AND NONE OF THE DRAWBACKS. IT'S THE CHEAPEST WAY TO GET OUR UNFILTERED VISION INTO AS MANY HANDS AS POSSIBLE!

VISION OF **WHAT,** PRECISELY?
GIRLS JUST WANT TO READ TRASHY ROMANCES THAT REMIND THEM OF SIMPLER TIMES.

COME ON, IT'S STUPID TO THINK THAT **ALL** WOMEN WANT TO READ THE SAME THING.
YOU'RE RIGHT THAT NOT EVERYTHING WE DO HAS TO HAVE SOME KIND OF SOCIAL AGENDA, BUT THAT DOESN'T MEAN IT CAN ONLY BE ANESTHETIZING CRAP.

WE COULD CREATE SOMETHING NEW, SOMETHING THAT CHALLENGES OUR AUDIENCE AT THE SAME TIME IT'S HELPING THEM **ESCAPE.**
ARTISTS ARE SUPPOSED TO HOLD A MIRROR UP TO SOCIETY, BUT OURS COULD BE A...A FUCKED-UP **FUNHOUSE** MIRROR!

WHAT IN GOD'S NAME ARE YOU TALKING ABOUT?

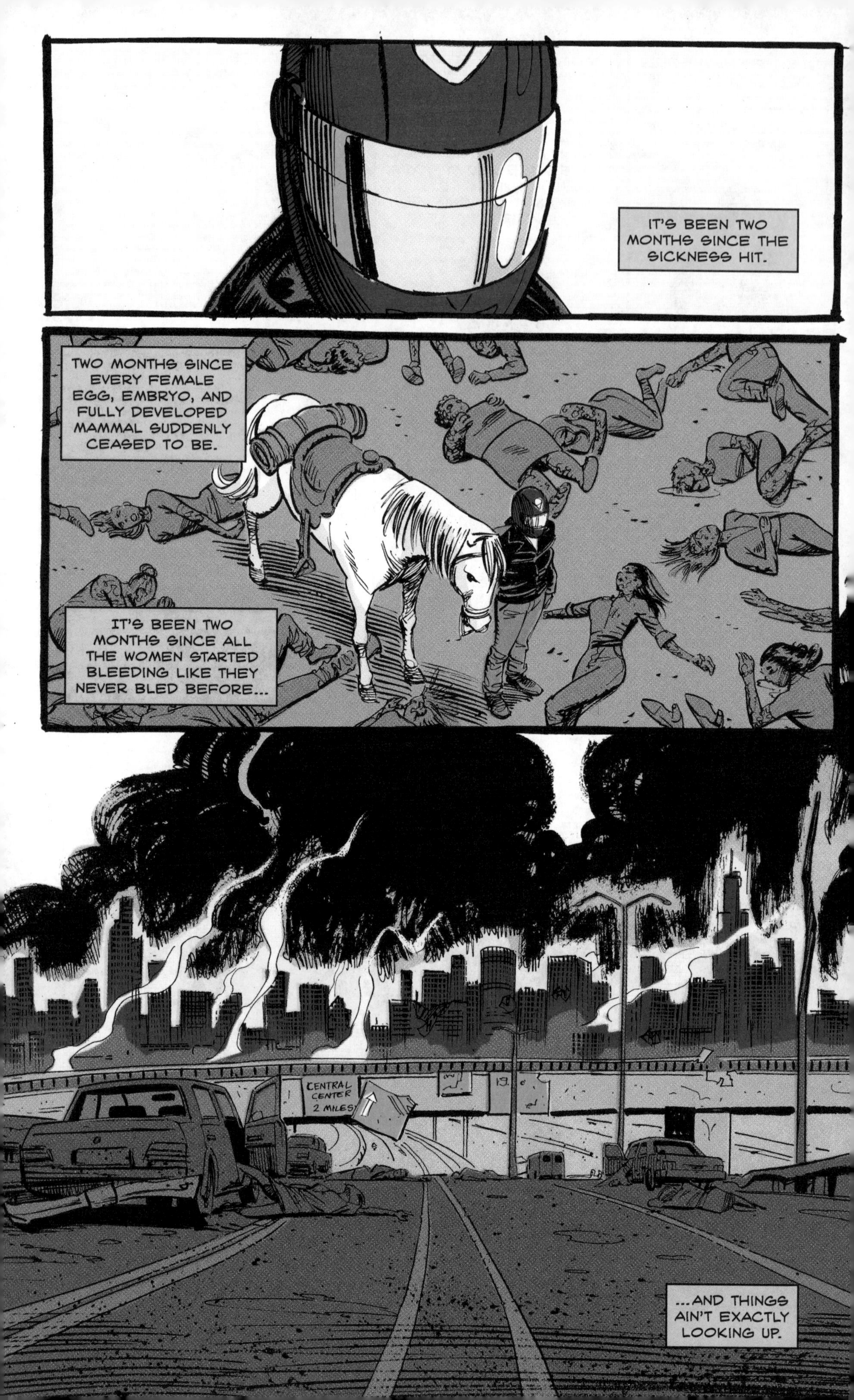
IT'S BEEN TWO MONTHS SINCE THE SICKNESS HIT.
TWO MONTHS SINCE EVERY FEMALE EGG, EMBRYO, AND FULLY DEVELOPED MAMMAL SUDDENLY CEASED TO BE.
IT'S BEEN TWO MONTHS SINCE ALL THE WOMEN STARTED BLEEDING LIKE THEY NEVER BLED BEFORE...
CENTRAL CENTER 2 MILES
...AND THINGS AIN'T EXACTLY LOOKING UP.

WHO KNEW THE WORLD WOULD CRUMBLE SO QUICKLY JUST BECAUSE 98% OF THE SECRETARIES AND KINDERGARTEN TEACHERS DIED?
WHO WOULD'VE GUESSED THAT SOCIETY WOULD COLLAPSE WITHOUT NURSES OR MAIDS OR WAITRESSES OR FREAKIN' *LIBRARIANS?*

BUT IT TURNS OUT THAT THESE COLD LITTLE BODIES WERE MORE THAN JUST OPERATORS, MORE THAN JUST RECEPTIONISTS.
THEY WERE EVEN MORE THAN MOTHERS AND WIVES AND SISTERS.

IF THE LAST SIXTY DAYS ARE ANY INDICATION, THESE LADIES WERE HOLDING UP THEIR HALF OF THE SKY AND THEN SOME.
I RECKON THEY WERE THE ONLY THING PREVENTING THE BOYS FROM BEATING EACH OTHER INTO OBLIVION AND THEN RAPING THE CORPSES.

*NEEEIGH*
I DON'T KNOW WHY EITHER, AIRHEART.

# FISH & BICYCLE COMIXX PRESENTS:

# I Am Woman

CAYCE B. SHELDON & HENRIETTA SPENCER
STORY ART

**Beijing, China**
**Now**

I HEARD IT'S THE BESTSELLING SERIES SINCE OLD-SCHOOL SUPERMAN BACK IN THE 1940s.
ALTHOUGH "BESTSELLING" IS RELATIVE, ESPECIALLY WHEN THE COVER PRICE IS, "WHATEVER DONATION YOU AND YOUR SHOPKEEPER FEEL IS FAIR."
WHAT'S IT ABOUT? SUPERWOMAN?
IT'S SUPERGIRL, 355.
AND NO, THIS ISN'T A CAPES-AND-TIGHTS BOOK. IT'S THIS QUASI-FEMINIST SCI-FI THING. VERY PO-MO.
IF YOU WERE AN ENGLISH MAJOR, WHY CAN'T YOU SPEAK ENGLISH?
IS IT ANY GOOD OR NOT?

MEH.
TO BE CONTINUED...

Moscow, The United Soviet States
Now

THE BEATLE?
NO, IDIOT, THE--
THAT WAS A JOKE, 355.

AND I THINK YOUR TURTLENECK IS ON TOO TIGHT. I MEAN, COMRADE GOATEE IS CHILLING IN HIS TOMB IN RED SQUARE, NOT RIDING FREIGHT WITH US.
THEY MUST HAVE DECIDED TO MOVE HIM.
WHY?

THEY SHIPPED HIS CORPSE TO KUIBYSHEV IN '41, WHEN IT LOOKED LIKE THE KREMLIN MIGHT FALL TO THE NAZIS.
МОСКВА
MAYBE THEY'RE TRYING TO GET HIM AWAY FROM ALL THE REACTOR MELTDOWNS NATALYA WARNED US ABOUT.

I FIGURE THE RUSSIANS BURNED ALL THEIR PLAGUE VICTIMS LIKE EVERYONE ELSE DID, SO VLADIMIR HERE IS PROBABLY THE BEST-PRESERVED MALE ON THE PLANET.
PRESENT COMPANY EXCLUDED, OF COURSE.

EXACTLY, SO IF THIS WERE REALLY THE REAL DUDE, WHY WOULD HE JUST BE HANGING OUT IN A BOX WITHOUT ANY GUARDS TO--
NYE DVIGUYT'YES!

⟨WHO THE HELL ARE YOU?⟩

AH. ARMED GOONS.
AWESOME.
⟨PLEASE TO BE EXCUSE US. MY GIRLFRIEND AND I ONLY WANTS TO, ER, PAYS US RESPECTING TO YOUR--⟩

DAVOL'NA!
⟨SEARCH THE SKINNY BITCH. SHE'S PROBABLY WORKING FOR THE CHECHENS.⟩

THERE'S NO WAY I'M LETTING THESE GYPSY ASSHOLES STEAL BETH'S ENGAGEMENT RING, THREE-FIFTY.
I DIDN'T SURVIVE THIS LONG TO SHOW UP EMPTY-HANDED.
JUST BE COOL, 'RICK.

⟨PLEASE, WE ARE FRIENDS TO YOUR COUNTRY. MY ASSISTANT AND I IS COLLEAGUES WITH FELLOW SOLDIER TO YOUSE PEOPLES, A WOMAN SNIPER NAMED--⟩
⟨SHUT YOUR BLACK MOUTH.⟩

VAAT IS THIS?

FUCK COMMUNISM

OH, THAT! IT'S FROM A COMIC BOOK!
HEH.

⟨THEY'RE REBELS, COMMANDANT.⟩
⟨OBVIOUSLY.⟩
⟨KILL THEM BOTH.⟩

SIGH
THINK

I TOLD YOU TO GET RID OF THAT DAMN LIGHTER!
NHK!

THAT'S NOT WHAT YOU SAID WHEN IT SAVED OUR BACON IN ULAN BATOR!
UNF!

KRACK
HURRY, THERE'LL BE MORE WHERE THESE THREE CAME FROM.

WE'RE ABANDONING SHIP? WHEN WE'RE SO CLOSE?
WE WERE GONNA HAVE TO SWITCH LINES FOR THE PARIS LEG ANYWAY. GRAB AMPERSAND AND START MOVING FOR THE LAST CAR.
WE'RE NOT GONNA ***JUMP***, ARE WE?

AND BASH MY BRAINS OUT LIKE MARRISVILLE?
NO, I MADE OTHER ARRANGEMENTS.

GOT IT, WE'RE GONNA DISCONNECT THE CABOOSE FROM THE REST OF THE TRAIN, RIGHT?
THIS IS THE TRANS-SIBERIAN RAILROAD, NOT A ***LIONEL SET***. I ***WISH*** IT WERE AS EASY AS UNHOOKING A LATCH.
SO HOW ARE WE GETTING OUT OF HERE?

MAGIC.

MOCBVA
MOCBVA

HUH, CHINESE GUNPOWDER REALLY DOES HAVE MORE KICK THAN THE AMERICAN STUFF.
GOOD TO KNOW.
WHAT?

NICE PUNCH BACK THERE, BY THE WAY.
YOU FINALLY LEARNED TO STOP HITTING LIKE A GIRL.
YEAH, WELL...

...I HAD A VERY MANLY INSTRUCTOR.
MOCBVA

**Paris, France**
**Now**

JESUS, WILL SOMEONE PLEASE SHUT THAT KID UP?
THAT KID IS MY SON, HERO.
YOU KNOW, THE NEXT-TO-LAST OF HIS KIND?

CIBA, I LET YOU AND NATALYA STAY WITH US UNDER THE CONDITION THAT YOU'D HELP ME FIND MY BROTHER, NOT ANNOY THE LIVING SHIT OUT OF ME.

THAT'S NOT FAIR, HERO.
OTHER-BETH IS CORRECT.
WE BUST OUR ASSHOLES LOOKING FOR YORICK ALL NOON LONG.

YEAH, WHILE I WAS STUCK HERE BABYSITTING.
THE ISRAELI MILITARY IS STILL OUT THERE, PEOPLE. IT'S TIME WE STOP ACTING LIKE A GODDAMN DAYCARE, AND START ACTING LIKE AN ARMY OURSELVES.

WHEN I WAS WITH THE DAUGHTERS OF THE AMAZON, IT TOOK US LESS THAN A MONTH TO TRACK DOWN YORICK, AND HE WAS HALFWAY ACROSS THE FUCKING COUNTRY!
SO WHAT, YOU WANT US TO START BEHAVING LIKE SAVAGES, HERO?
LIKE YOU USED TO?

I'M... I'M SORRY. I DIDN'T MEAN THAT.
RELAX, NASA. I'M THE ONE WHO SHOULD BE APOLOGIZING.
I DON'T KNOW WHAT THE HELL IS WRONG WITH ME.

I WATCH BETH BREASTFEED, AND IT MAKES MY MASTECTOMY SCAR ACHE. ALL I HAVE TO SHOW FOR MY LIFE IS A FUCKING SOCK STUFFED IN MY BRA, LIKE I'M FOURTEEN ALL OVER AGAIN.
OH, HONEY...
IT'S TRUE. YOU HAVE BETH JUNIOR, CIBA HAS BABY VLAD...EVEN NATALYA HAS HER STUPID RIFLE.

HIS NAME IS RODYA.
AFTER MY HUSBAND.

ALL OF US GIRLS LOSE SOMETHING IN THIS WAR, HEROIC.

BUT MAYBE WE EACH GETS SOMETHING, TOO.

IT'S GONE!

YOU IN THERE, AGENT 355?
LOOK, WHEN WE GOT ON BOARD, I THINK I LOST MY...

...PRECIOUS?

CRAP, UM, SORRY, I WAS JUST--
SHH, CLOSE THE DOOR BEHIND YOU.

BUT YOU'RE...
NOTHING YOU HAVEN'T SEEN BEFORE, RIGHT? STANDARD-ISSUE UNDERTHINGS FOR WHEN US CULPER RING GIRLS DO AN INTERVENTION.
INTERVENTION? WHAT FOR?

I'M YOUR FRIEND, AREN'T I?
YOU'RE, LIKE, MY BEST FRIEND.
THEN I HAVE TO TELL YOU YOU'RE MAKING A TERRIBLE MISTAKE.

WHAT DOES THAT MEAN?
YOU ALREADY KNOW...

...THAT YOU'RE GONNA DIE IF YOU COME FOR ME.

NUHFUCK!

GOOD LORD, I WOULD HATE TO SPEND A NIGHT IN YOUR HEAD.
SORRY, I HAD THIS HORRIBLE--
PLEASE, WE'RE ALMOST THROUGH GERMANY. I'D LOVE TO MAKE IT ACROSS ONE COUNTRY WITHOUT BEING BORED BY EVERY DETAIL OF YOUR BATSHIT DREAMS.
TSS

IF I ASK YOU SOMETHING, DO YOU PROMISE TO ANSWER HONESTLY?
PROBABLY NOT.
MEDECINS SANS FRONTIERES
MEDECINS SANS FRONTIERES
MEDECINS SANS FRONTIERES
MEDECINS SANS FRONTIERES

AM I GOING BALD?

THE HELL?
JUST TELL ME THE TRUTH, I CAN TAKE IT!
I DON'T KNOW. I GUESS IT'S...THINNED A BIT SINCE I FIRST MET YOU.

ASSFUCK! I KNEW IT!
AND I'M BARELY TWENTY-SEVEN! MY DAD HAD A FULL HEAD OF HAIR HIS ENTIRE LIFE!

GENETICS IS A CRAPSHOOT. YOU'RE THE SOLE SURVIVOR OF AN APOCALYPTIC PLAGUE, BUT YOUR HAIRLINE IS RECEDING.
WIN SOME, LOSE SOME.

SCREW IT, I'LL JUST SHAVE MY HEAD.
YEAH, DON'T DO THAT. WHITE BOYS LOOK LIKE SHIT BALD.
NOT SEAN CONNERY! YOU'D BONE SEAN CONNERY, RIGHT? YOU'RE A SPY FOR CHRIST'S SAKE!

YORICK, WHAT IS THIS ABOUT?

I HAVEN'T SEEN BETH IN FIVE YEARS. THAT'S LONGER THAN SHE AND I DATED!
WHAT IF SHE ISN'T...YOU KNOW, ATTRACTED TO ME ANYMORE?

WHAT DO YOU CARE? IT'S NOT LIKE THERE ARE OTHER FISH IN THE SEA FOR HER.
WILL YOU CALM DOWN? YOU'RE A DECENT GUY, YORICK BROWN. THAT WAS A RARITY EVEN BEFORE THE PLAGUE HIT.
WOW, THANKS, DEAR ABBY.

BESIDES, HOW DO YOU KNOW YOU'RE STILL GOING TO BE ATTRACTED TO HER?
I MEAN, I'VE GOTTEN FAT AS A HOUSE SINCE THE BOYS DIED.

OH, SHUT UP. YOU'RE TOTALLY HOTTER NOW THAN WHEN I FIRST GOT SADDLED WITH YOU.
YOU WERE ALL BUTCH AND SCARY BACK THEN. YOU'RE WAY MORE... WOMANLY THESE DAYS.

DO YOURSELF A FAVOR.
CHOOSE YOUR WORDS MORE CAREFULLY IF YOUR GIRL'S ASS HAS GOTTEN BIGGER.

PLEASE DON'T BREAK ME.

TIME TO SPAR, BIG MAN. YOU CAN'T CALL YOURSELF AN ESCAPE ARTIST IF YOU STILL DON'T KNOW HOW TO GET OUT OF A HEADLOCK.
YOU'RE GONNA HAVE TO START PROTECTING YOURSELF SOON, SO I WANT TO TEACH YOU AS MANY TRICKS OF THE TRADE AS I CAN BEFORE WE HEAD OUR SEPARATE WAYS.
I TOLD YOU, THREE-FIFTY, YOU SHOULD HANG WITH BETH AND ME FOR A WHILE. YOU TWO WOULD LOVE EACH OTHER.

THANKS, BUT IT'S TIME FOR ME TO MOVE ON.
REMEMBER YOUR STANCE.
SO YOU'RE GOING TO FIND YET ANOTHER NEEDY SOUL TO BE GUARDIAN ANGEL TO?

YOU HAVE A BETTER IDEA?

YOU DESERVE TO BE SO MUCH MORE THAN AN "ESCORT," 355.
THIS IS GOING TO SOUND CORNBALL, BUT YOU SHOULD TAKE A LITTLE TIME TO FIND YOURSELF.
HUH, YOU'RE ACTUALLY KINDA RIGHT...

...THAT DOES SOUND CORNBALL.
OOF!

I'M...SERIOUS. GET OUT THERE... AND ENJOY THE WORLD. I MEAN, YOU HAVEN'T SEEN A MOVIE OR ...OR BOUGHT A CD SINCE YOU WERE TWELVE.
YOU'VE SPENT MOST OF YOUR LIFE JUST THINKING ABOUT THE DUDES YOU'VE BEEN PROTECTING.

I'M SUPPOSED TO TAKE ADVICE ON BEING TOO FOCUSED ON SOMEONE ELSE FROM YOU?
HEY, MY RELATIONSHIP WITH BETH IS PERFECTLY HEALTH--

--EEEUNF!

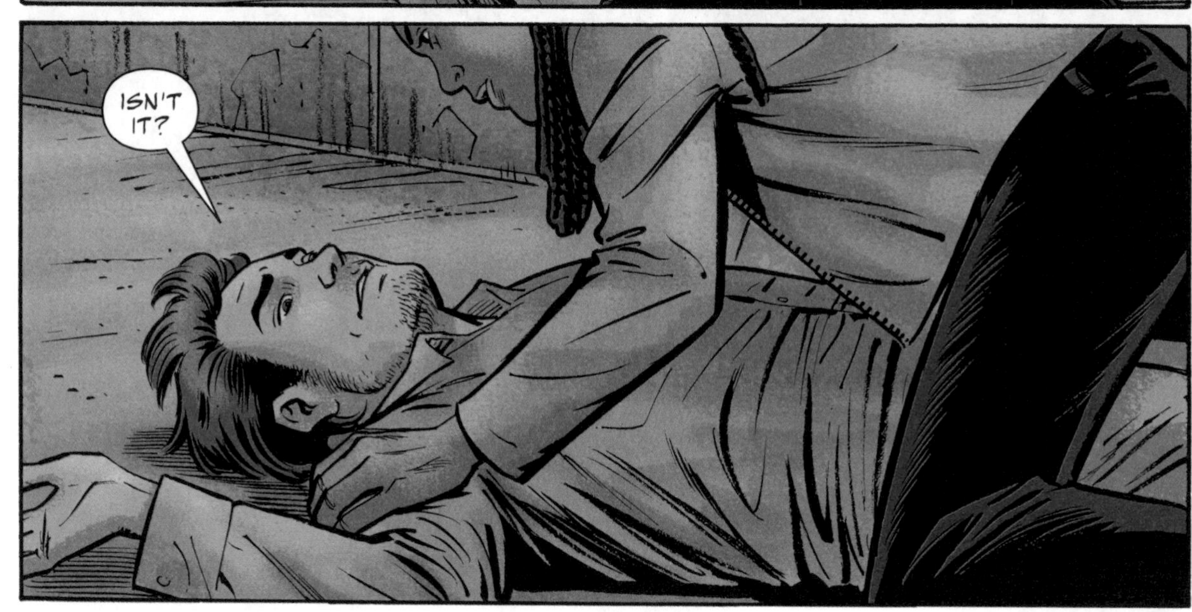
ISN'T IT?

HELL IF I KNOW, BUT AT LEAST YOU'VE FIGURED OUT HOW TO COLLAPSE SAFELY.
SERIOUSLY, WHAT'S YOUR DEFINITION OF "HEALTHY"?
FACTORING IN FORCED SEPARATION, MASS EXTINCTION AND OTHER SPECTACULARLY MITIGATING CIRCUMSTANCES, OF COURSE.

MY MOM ONCE TOLD ME THAT A GOOD RELATIONSHIP ISN'T WHERE THE OTHER PERSON MAKES YOU FEEL BETTER, BUT WHERE THEY MAKE YOU BETTER.
YOURS FIT THAT BILL?

WELL, I USED TO BE A SELF-CENTERED, SUICIDAL SHUT-IN.
BUT THESE DAYS, I FLATTER MYSELF TO THINK I'M A WHOLE DIFFERENT STRING OF ALLITERATION.

AND THAT'S ALL BECAUSE OF HER, RIGHT?

<SON OF A BITCH.>

<IS THERE ONE SYNAGOGUE THESE ANTI-SEMITIC ANIMALS DIDN'T BURN TO THE GROUND AFTER THE SICKNESS HIT?>

<IF ANY OF YOU STILL QUESTION WHY WE'RE SPENDING TIME AND RESOURCES SEARCHING FOR THE LAST BOY, JUST DIRTY YOUR HANDS IN THOSE ASHES.>

<THE WORLD IS STILL ACHING TO FINISH WHAT THE NAZIS STARTED, AND SECURING A LIVING MALE BEFORE OUR ENEMIES CAN IS THE ONLY LEVERAGE WE HAVE TO ENSURE OUR NATION'S CONTINUED SURVI-->
ALTER!

<I MEAN, **LIEUTENANT-GENERAL.**>
<FORGIVE ME, I JUST-->
<WHAT IS IT, PRIVATE?>

<I THINK I HAVE A LEAD, MA'AM.>
<ON YORICK?>
<NO, ON THE **GIRL** HE'S AFTER.>

<I WAS OVER AT CLEOPATRA'S NEEDLE, AND I HEARD THAT A **BLONDE GIRL** WAS THERE TODAY.>
<SHE WAS LOOKING FOR A **MAN.**>

<**EVERY** WOMAN IN THIS HELLHOLE IS LOOKING FOR A MAN, ELIANA.>
<**ESPECIALLY** THE BLONDES.>
<I KNOW, BUT THIS ONE LEFT SOMETHING BEHIND.>

<HN.>
<COLLECT YOUR THINGS, LADIES.>

⟨WE'RE ON THE MARCH.⟩
WHYS AND WHEREFORES

PARIS

Paris, France
Now

WE'RE FINALLY CLOSE TO FINDING THE WOMAN YOU'VE TRAVELED 25,000 MILES FOR, AND ALL YOU CAN THINK ABOUT IS *DESSERT?*

BETH IS A MASSIVE CHOCOHOLIC, TOO, THREE-FIFTY.
IF WE CHILL HERE LONG ENOUGH, WE MIGHT SEE HER OR...OR SOMEBODY WHO *KNOWS* HER.
BUT WE'RE ALMOST OUT OF EUROS, 'RICK. AND IF IT'S POSSIBLE FOR THE TWO OF US TO LOOK *MORE* SUSPICIOUS, IT'LL BE BY HANGING OUT HERE WITH-OUT *BUYING* SOMETHING.

I DON'T THINK WE HAVE TO. MY FRANÇAIS IS A LITTLE RUSTY, BUT I'M PRETTY SURE THIS THING SAYS...
"AS A NATURAL ANTIDEPRESSANT... LE CHOCOLAT IS... SOMETHING SOMETHING SOMETHING...AND SO, THE PARLIAMENT OFFERS...DAILY RATION TO ALL WOMEN...FREE OF CHARGE!"

SEE, THE BROTHERS MAY BE DEAD, BUT FRATERNITÉ IS ALIVE AND WELL.
FINE.
I SUPPOSE WE CAN GRAB *ONE PIECE.*

A MOMENT ON THE FUCKIN' LIPS...
PAT

THIS IS POINTLESS.

WHAT ARE YOU TALKING ABOUT, HERO? FIVE MINUTES AGO, YOU SAID YOU COULD FEEL THAT YORICK WAS CLOSE.
THAT WAS JUST BULLSHIT TO KEEP YOU GUYS ON THE HUNT, CIBA.
I'M SO SORRY ABOUT THIS, DRAGGING YOU AND YOUR SON ACROSS THE ENTIRE GODDAMN PLANET.

HEY, CIRCLING THE GLOBE IS OLD HAT FOR ME, REMEMBER? BESIDES, I LOVE TREKKING WITH YOU GUYS.
VLAD MAY BE MY WORLD NOW, BUT I DIDN'T ENDURE THREE YEARS OF PAYLOAD SPECIALIST TRAINING TO SIT INSIDE A MINIVAN AND PLAY SOCCER MOM ALL DAY.
<FUCKING MIDGET BASTARD.>

<YOUR COUNTRYWOMEN SHOULD HAVE RIPPED DOWN THESE LITTLE MONUMENTS BACK IN 1812, AFTER YOU DRAGGED THEIR HUSBANDS TO BLEED ALL OVER MY SOIL.>
YOU'RE MUTTERING IN RUSSIAN AGAIN, NATALYA, SO IF YOU'RE SWEARING AT ME, IT'S FALLING ON DEAF--
YORICK!

UM... *WHERE?*
IT'S... IT'S *REALLY* HIM.

THERE.
AVEZ-VOUS VU CET HOMME?

CRAP, SOMEBODY RIPPED OFF THE *CONTACT INFO.*
NO MATTERS, THIS IS STILL A VERY EXCELLED CLUE ON FINDING LAST MAN AND HIS BETH NUMBER TWO!

ACTUALLY, IN YORICK'S EYES, SHE'S *BETH NUMBER ONE.*
AND SHE'S... SHE'S *PRETTY,* HUH?

DON'T BE HILARIOUS, ELIZABETH.
SHE IS NICE GIRL, BUT YOU ARE BEAUTIFUL WOMAN. YOUR FACE HAS MORE... CHARACTERISTICS.

THANKS, NAT, BUT IT'S NOT A COMPETITION.
I MAY HAVE BEEN THE JEZEBEL WHO STOLE YORICK FOR AN EVENING, BUT I'M NOT GONNA BE THE HOMEWRECKER WHO RUINS THINGS WITH THE POOR GUY'S TRUE LOVE.

HE'S THE FATHER OF YOUR DAUGHTER, BETH.
IT'S FINE IF YORICK'S BACK WITH DEVILLE NOW, BUT HE'S GOING TO FIND A WAY TO MAKE YOU AND BETH JUNIOR A PART OF HIS LIFE, TOO.
THAT'S NOT HIS RESPONSIBILITY, HERO. THIS BABY WAS MY CHOICE. WHAT IF YOUR BROTHER ISN'T READY TO BE A DAD?
AVEC
VOU
REN
CINE
527 RUE

EZ-VOUS
ET HOMME?
ESTIVAL
THEN I WILL TEACH HIM THE MEANING OF DEADBEAT.

METROPOLITAIN
DON'T JUST SHOVE IT IN!

GENTLE NOW. THAT'S IT, NIIIIIICE AND SLOW.
POUNDING AWAY ISN'T GOING TO GET THE JOB DONE, YOU HAVE TO USE FINESSE.

VOILÁ!
YOU JUST PICKED YOUR FIRST EUROPEAN DEADBOLT.
FANTASTIC, NOW GET YOUR ASS INSIDE.
Entrée des Catacombes

WAIT, WE'RE REALLY GOING DOWN THERE?
UNTIL I'M SURE YOUR GIRLFRIEND IS THE ONLY PERSON LOOKING FOR YOU, I THINK WE SHOULD KEEP OUR HEADS DOWN AT NIGHT.

THIS IS MY REPAYMENT FOR IMPARTING AN INVALUABLE BODY OF ESCAPOLOGIST KNOWLEDGE?
YOU MAKE ME SLEEP UNDER-GROUND?
YOU DIDN'T TEACH ME ALL YOUR TRICKS, YORICK.

WHAT ARE YOU TALKING ABOUT? WE WENT OVER HANDCUFFS, LEG IRONS, STRAIT-JACKETS...
HOW ABOUT THAT DISAPPEARING ACT YOU DID BACK AT THE WASHINGTON MONUMENT? I TURNED AROUND FOR A SECOND, AND YOU JUST VANISHED INTO THIN AIR.
YOU NEVER TOLD ME HOW.

YEAH, WELL, WHY DON'T YOU TELL ME WHAT HANDLE YOU WENT BY BEFORE YOU WERE A NUMERAL, AND THEN I'LL SPILL THE BEANS.

WE'VE BEEN OVER THIS A MILLION TIMES.
MY OLD NAME WAS BORING. WHATEVER YOU IMAGINE IT WAS IS PROBABLY WAY MORE INTERESTING THAN THE TRUTH.
OKAY, THEN I CHOOSE TO BELIEVE YOU WERE CHRISTENED...RHODA McBLOWHOLE. MISS McBLOWHOLE IF YOU'RE...

...NASTY?

JESUS.
ARE THEY ALL...?
NO, THESE SKELETONS WERE DOWN HERE LONG BEFORE OUR PLAGUE HIT.
SO THESE ARE MEN AND WOMEN?
WELL, THEY WERE.
BUT YEAH, MALES AND FEMALES ALL GOT BURIED TOGETHER DOWN HERE.
HOW CAN ANYBODY TELL THE DIFFERENCE?

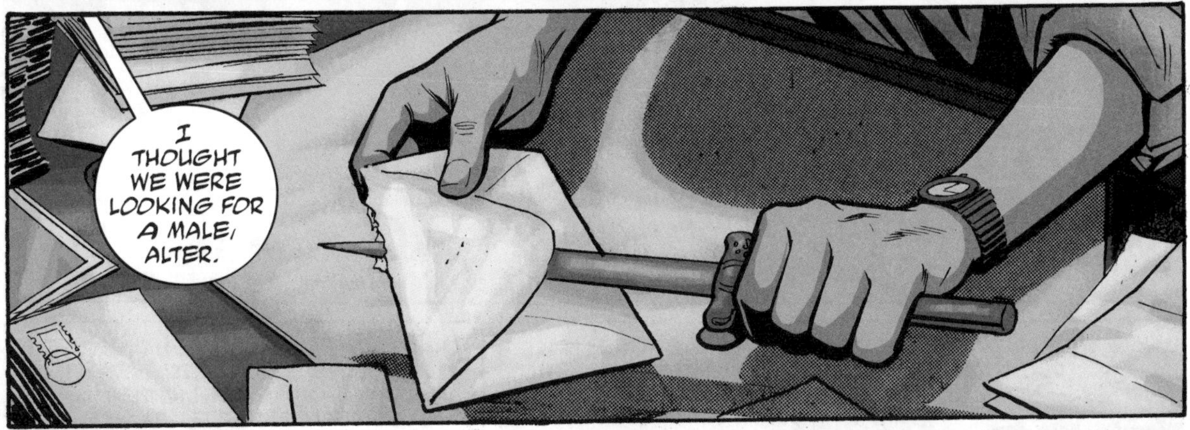
I THOUGHT WE WERE LOOKING FOR A MALE, ALTER.

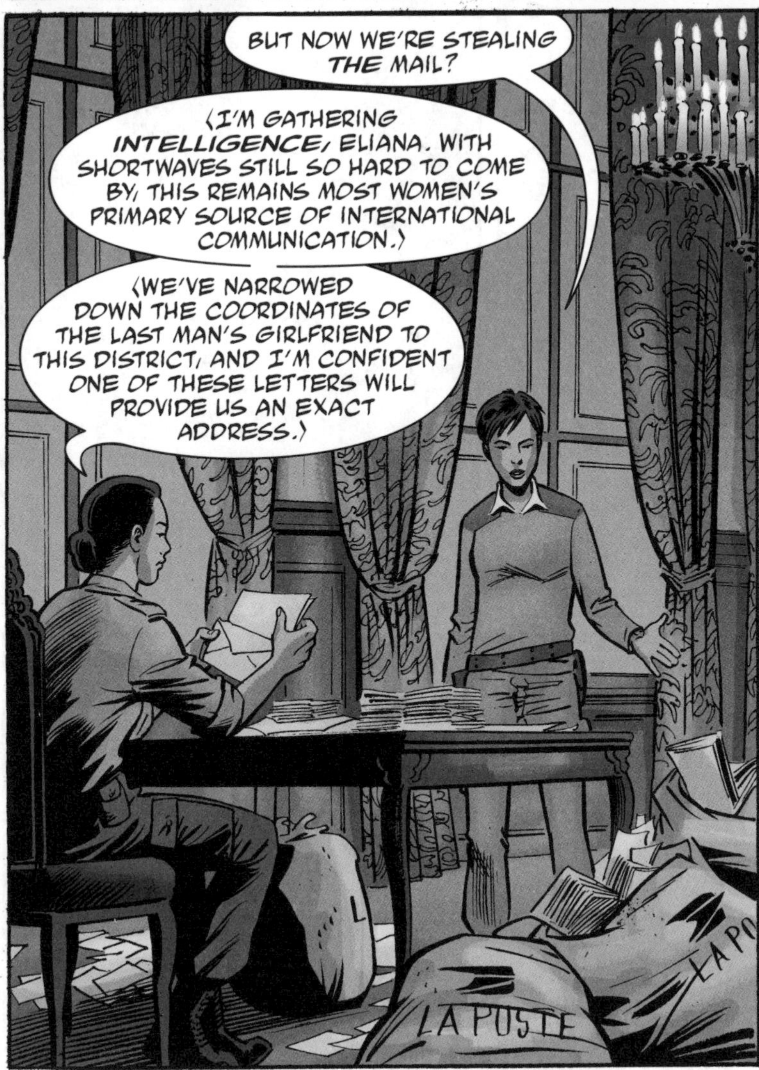
BUT NOW WE'RE STEALING THE MAIL?
⟨I'M GATHERING INTELLIGENCE, ELIANA. WITH SHORTWAVES STILL SO HARD TO COME BY, THIS REMAINS MOST WOMEN'S PRIMARY SOURCE OF INTERNATIONAL COMMUNICATION.⟩
⟨WE'VE NARROWED DOWN THE COORDINATES OF THE LAST MAN'S GIRLFRIEND TO THIS DISTRICT, AND I'M CONFIDENT ONE OF THESE LETTERS WILL PROVIDE US AN EXACT ADDRESS.⟩
LA POSTE
LA PO

⟨AND IF IT DOESN'T, I SUPPOSE YOU'LL BURN THE POST OFFICE TO THE GROUND, AS WELL?⟩

⟨I'M NOT SURE I UNDERSTAND WHAT YOU'RE SUGGESTING.⟩
⟨I'M NOT SUGGESTING ANYTHING. I KNOW, ALTER.⟩
⟨THAT SYNAGOGUE YOU CLAIM THE FRENCH BURNED DOWN AFTER THE MEN DIED? IT WAS YOU.⟩
⟨THAT'S WHAT HAPPENED TO THE LAST OF OUR FUEL RATION.⟩

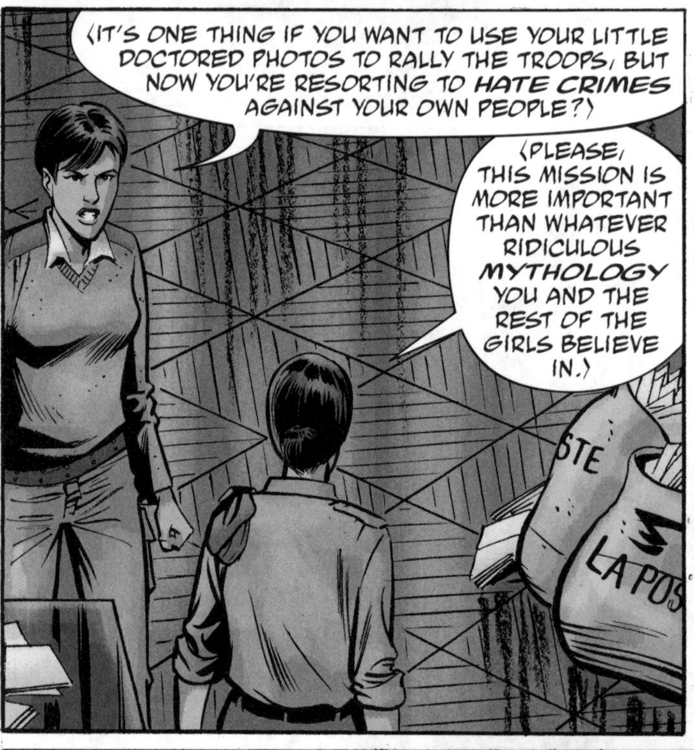
⟨IT'S ONE THING IF YOU WANT TO USE YOUR LITTLE DOCTORED PHOTOS TO RALLY THE TROOPS, BUT NOW YOU'RE RESORTING TO HATE CRIMES AGAINST YOUR OWN PEOPLE?⟩
⟨PLEASE, THIS MISSION IS MORE IMPORTANT THAN WHATEVER RIDICULOUS MYTHOLOGY YOU AND THE REST OF THE GIRLS BELIEVE IN.⟩
STE
LA POS

⟨AND THE PICTURES I SHOWED YOU WEREN'T DOCTORED. FEMALE PLATOONS FROM NORTH KOREA, CHILE AND OTHER COUNTRIES REALLY ARE AT WAR IN DIFFERENT CORNERS OF THE GLOBE.⟩
⟨THEY'RE JUST SQUABBLING OVER THE SAME PETTY THINGS ARMIES ALWAYS HAVE...LAND, RESOURCES, RELIGIOUS NONSENSE.⟩

⟨BUT YOU TOLD US WE HAD TO RESCUE THE LAST MAN BEFORE ANOTHER MILITARY GOT THEIR HANDS ON HIM.⟩
⟨IF THEY DON'T CARE ABOUT YORICK BROWN...WHY THE HELL DO YOU?⟩

⟨I'M DONE EXPLAINING MY STRATEGY TO YOU.⟩
⟨DONE? YOU HAVEN'T EVEN *STARTED.*⟩
⟨WHAT'S YOUR PLAN HERE? *REALLY?* I'VE DONE EVERYTHING YOU ASKED, AND I DESERVE TO...⟩

⟨...NO.⟩
⟨YOU'RE DISMISSED, PRIVATE.⟩

⟨TELL SADIE I SAID HELLO.⟩
LA POSTE

YOU FINALLY STARTING YOUR GREAT AMERICAN NOVEL?
NAH, THAT ONE'S STILL KIND OF IN THE...OUTLINE PHASE.
SO WHAT ARE YOU WORKING ON NOW?

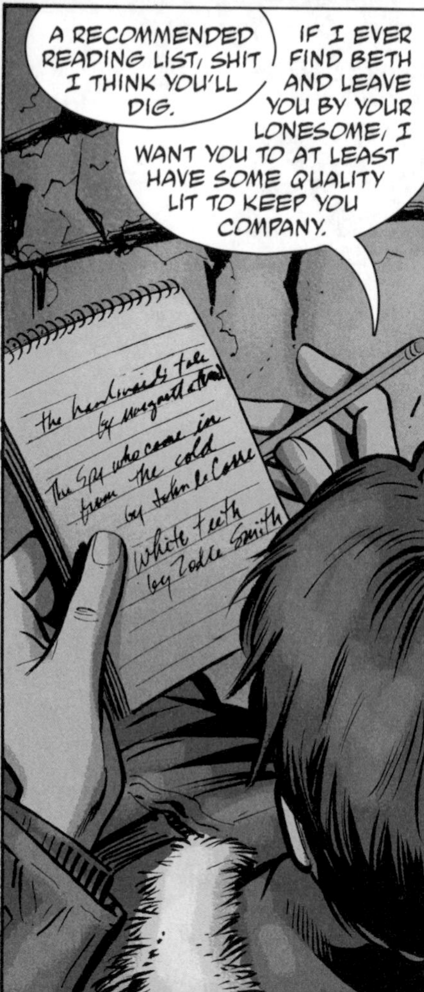
A RECOMMENDED READING LIST, SHIT I THINK YOU'LL DIG.
IF I EVER FIND BETH AND LEAVE YOU BY YOUR LONESOME, I WANT YOU TO AT LEAST HAVE SOME QUALITY LIT TO KEEP YOU COMPANY.

NOT IF, 'RICK.
WHEN YOU FIND BETH.

I SUPPOSE.
IT'S TRUE.
TRUST ME, YOU'LL TRACK HER DOWN AND LIVE HAPPILY EVER AFTER WITH YOUR FOURTEEN CHILDREN.

CHILDREN.

WHAT, YOU'RE NOT A BREEDER?
NO, I DEFINITELY AM. AT LEAST, I USED TO BE. USED TO WANT TO BE.
BUT THAT WAS BEFORE I BECAME THE LAST POTENTIAL PROUD PAPA. IF I EVER HAVE A SON, HOW THE FUCK AM I GOING TO TEACH HIM TO BE, YOU KNOW...MASCULINE?

YORICK, DO YOU KNOW HOW MANY OF THE CULPER RING'S BOSSES NEVER EVEN KNEW THEIR DADS?
THERE ARE PLENTY OF PRESIDENTS WHO GREW UP WITHOUT THEIR FATHERS IN THEIR LIVES AT ALL. JACKSON, GARFIELD, CLINTON...
...MILOSEVIC, AMIN, HUSSEIN...

THEY WEREN'T ALL GREAT MEN, BUT THEY WERE MEN.
GOOD OR BAD, IT'S ALWAYS BEEN WOMEN WHO'VE SHAPED BOYS INTO WHATEVER THE HELL IT IS THEY'RE GONNA BECOME.

HUH.

I WENT TO SCHOOL WITH THIS KID NAMED SULLY.
HE HAD ONE OF THOSE REALLY BAD PEANUT ALLERGIES, THE KIND THAT KILLS YOU DEAD IF YOU GOT A WHIFF OF A SINGLE REESE'S, YOU KNOW?
UM...?

ANYWAY, THE TEACHERS SET UP THIS SPECIAL TABLE FOR HIM, "THE PEANUT-ALLERGY TABLE" THEY EVEN CALLED IT.
YOU COULDN'T SIT THERE IF YOU HAD A PB&J OR WHATEVER IN YOUR BROWN BAG, SO SULLY ENDED UP EATING ALL BY HIMSELF. EVERY SINGLE DAY.

WHY DIDN'T YOU PACK A BALONEY SANDWICH?
HANG OUT WITH THE POOR KID?
I DON'T KNOW. RULES OF THE CHALKBOARD JUNGLE, I GUESS.

BUT I NEVER FELT *BAD* ABOUT IT UNTIL I MET YOU.

OH. SORRY...?
NO, IT'S A GOOD THING.
I MEAN, I NEVER KNEW WHAT IT MUST HAVE FELT LIKE TO BE SULLY UNTIL THE PLAGUE HIT.
AND I NEVER KNEW THE KIND OF PERSON EXISTED WHO WOULD HAVE SAT NEXT TO HIM UNTIL YOU CAME ALONG.
ANYWAY.
SLEEP TIGHT, DUDE.
YEAH.
YOU, TOO.

UGH, BACK HERE AGAIN?
THIS IS THE FIFTH TIME SINCE WE GOT TO TOWN.
I KNOW, BUT I DID A LITTLE EARLY-MORNING RECON WHILE YOU WERE ASLEEP. THINK I MIGHT HAVE A LEAD.

A LEAD?
ON BETH? HOW DID YOU--

LOOK, I'VE BEEN DOING THIS A LONG TIME, BUT THERE'S ONE PART OF THE JOB I STILL SUCK AT.
SO I'M JUST GONNA DO IT...

WHAT ARE YOU--
THIS IS FOR YOU.

SORRY I DIDN'T HAVE TIME TO WRAP IT.

THIS...THIS IS YOUR SCARF.
YOU'VE BEEN KNITTING THIS THING FOR ALMOST, LIKE, FIVE YEARS.
WELL, I FUCKED UP A LOT, SO I HAD TO START OVER A BUNCH OF TIMES.

YOU'RE GIVING THIS TO ME?
I KNOW HOW MUCH YOU HATE HAVING TO SHAVE EVERY MORNING, AND I FIGURE THIS'LL BE A MORE PRACTICAL WAY TO HIDE YOUR STUBBLE THAN THAT SMELLY OLD GASMASK.
BUT... WHY NOW?

JUST AS A THANK-YOU, 'RICK.
FOR...YOU KNOW.

BUT I'M THE ONE WHO SHOULD BE THANKING...

355?

THREE-FIFTY?

THREE-FIFTY!

YORICK?

YORICK BROWN?

BETH?

NO.
NO, FUCK YOU.
WHAT?

THIS IS A DREAM. I'M STILL ASLEEP IN THE CATACOMBS, HAVING ANOTHER FUCKING DREAM.
YORICK, LOOK AT ME.
LOOK AT ME.

THIS ISN'T A DREAM.

**Paris, France**
***Maintenant***

OH, JE REGARDE JUSTE. VOTRE TRAVAIL EST SUPERBE.
AH, AMERICAN. AND THANK YOU. YOU HAVE GOOD TASTE.
MY FATHER WAS A TAILOR.
REALLY? MINE, TOO.

I LOVE THIS ONE.
EST-CE QUE JE PEUX VOUS DEMANDER COMBIEN?

QUATRE CENTS EUROS POUR CETTE PIÈCE.
OR WHATEVER YOU HAVE TO BARTER, OF COURSE.

WELL...

NON! S'IL-VOUS-PLAÎT!
JUST TAKE IT!

WHAT?
OH! OH, NO.

I'M OFFERING TO EXCHANGE THIS.
I DON'T KNOW WHAT YOUR GUN LAWS ARE LIKE THESE DAYS, BUT--
HM, I HAVE BEEN ROBBED TWICE SINCE LE GRAND DÉPART.

IS IT EASY TO USE?

OUI.

TOO EASY.

HHHHNN

AAAHHN

WOW.

WHEN DID YOU GET THAT GOOD?

WHAT IS *THAT* SUPPOSED TO MEAN?
I'M KIDDING, YORICK.
MOSTLY.

SERIOUSLY, DO YOU REMEMBER THE TIME WE WERE SIXTY-NINING AND YOU KNEED ME IN THE FACE?
I HAD A CHARLEY HORSE!
YOU KNOW HOW EASILY I CRAMP!

AND YOU'RE THE ONE WHO *FARTED* THE VERY FIRST TIME WE HAD SEX!
THAT WASN'T A FART!
IT WAS YOUR SQUEAKY GODDAMN FUTON!

I MISSED YOU, BETH DEVILLE.
BETH NÉE DEVILLE.

UNLESS YOU WANT ME TO GIVE THIS BACK.

YOU'RE REALLY GOING TO TAKE MY NAME?
ISN'T THAT KIND OF... OLD-FASHIONED?
YORICK, YOU'RE THE ONLY MAN ON THE PLANET. ANYTHING I DO WITH YOU IS POSITIVELY FUTURISTIC.

POINT.
GOOD, NOW GET YOUR HUSBANDLY ASS OVER HERE AND GIVE ME MY PROPERS.

NOT UNTIL YOU FINISH WHAT YOU STARTED TELLING ME.
WHEN?
ON THE PHONE. RIGHT BEFORE THE PLAGUE HIT. THE *LAST* TIME I GOT DOWN ON BENDED KNEE. YOU SAID YOU HAD SOMETHING IMPORTANT YOU NEEDED TO TELL ME.

YORICK, WE HAVE FIVE YEARS OF CATCHING UP TO DO. WE DON'T HAVE TO DO IT ALL TONIGHT.
BESIDES, YOU'VE ONLY TOLD ME *HALF* THE STORIES BEHIND ALL YOUR MANLY NEW SCARS AND--

EEEEET
YAHH!

CAREFUL!
IF YOU LOOK HIM DIRECTLY IN THE EYE, HE'LL CLAW YOU A NEW NOSTRIL!

RELAX, YORICK.
AMPERSAND IS CRAZY ABOUT ME.
HUH. HE ACTUALLY *IS.*

THIS LITTLE GUY IS REALLY WHO I HAVE TO THANK FOR YOU STILL BEING HERE, HUH?
I GUESS SO. ALONG WITH MY FRIEND DR. MANN'S *FATHER.*
TURNS OUT THE CRAP THAT SAVED ME IS CONNECTED TO WHAT *CAUSED* THE GENDERCIDE. MONKEYS AND CLONES AND...SOME KIND OF MORPHING THING.

AS FAR AS ANSWERS GO, IT WAS...VAGUELY UNSATISFYING.

AFTER EVERYTHING WE'VE BEEN THROUGH?
IS THERE ANY EXPLANATION THAT WOULD HAVE BEEN *SATISFACTORY?*

UM, ALIENS?
I ALSO WOULD HAVE ACCEPTED WITCHCRAFT OR ANYTHING INVOLVING NANOBOTS.
BUT THAT'S KIND OF NOT THE POINT, RIGHT?

SORRY?
I'M JUST SAYING, IN THE END, IT'S NOT IMPORTANT WHAT KILLED THE MEN, ONLY WHAT THE REST OF US ARE GOING TO DO NOW THAT THEY'RE GONE.

THAT'S BULLSHIT, BETH.
THE PAST MATTERS. IT MATTERS A FUCKING LOT!

OKAY THEN.

SORRY. I...I DIDN'T MEAN TO FREAK OUT.
IT'S JUST, YOU'RE THE GENIUS ANTHROPOLOGIST HERE, SO I WAS KIND OF HOPING YOU'D HELP ENLIGHTEN ME ABOUT, YOU KNOW...WHY ALL THIS NEEDED TO HAPPEN.
WELL, WHAT IF IT'S NOT *WHY* IT HAPPENED...BUT *IF* IT EVEN DID?

THE WOMEN I SPENT TIME WITH IN THE OUTBACK, THEY'RE CONVINCED THIS HAS SOMETHING TO DO WITH THE *DREAMTIME.*
THEY THINK OUR CREATIVE FOREFATHERS HAVE FALLEN ASLEEP, SO ALL THE MEN HAVE JUST TEMPORARILY JOINED THEM IN A STREAM OF REALITY THAT RUNS PARALLEL TO OUR OWN.

I KNOW HOW IT SOUNDS, BUT DREAMS ARE WHAT TOLD ME THAT YOU WERE STILL ALIVE, YORICK. DREAMS ARE HOW I *FOUND* YOU.
YOU HAVE TO ADMIT, SOMETHING BIGGER THAN *HAPPENSTANCE* REUNITED US.

HN.

YOU THINK I'M INSANE, DON'T YOU?
YOU LIKING STAR WARS MORE THAN 2001 IS *INSANE.*
THIS IS JUST... ECCENTRIC.

I GUESS I DON'T PLACE MUCH STOCK IN THE UNCONSCIOUS MIND.
EVER SINCE I STARTED LOOKING FOR YOU, I'VE BEEN HAVING THESE NIGHTMARES TELLING ME THAT I *SHOULDN'T.*

OH.

NO, THAT'S WHAT I'M TRYING TO TELL YOU! *MY* DREAMS WERE *MEANINGLESS!*
SOMETIMES, A CIGAR IS JUST A MOUTHFUL OF SMOLDERING PHALLIC SYMBOL. NOT EVERYTHING HAS A HIDDEN--
CEE

CEEEEE

NICE. CONGRESSWOMAN BROWN KNIT THAT FOR YOU?
NAH, A GIRL I KNOW.
A...A WOMAN.

RIGHT.
OH, COME ON! IT'S NOT LIKE THAT!
YORICK, IT'S FINE. YOU DON'T NEED TO EXPLAIN.
I DO! ABOUT A LOT OF THINGS.

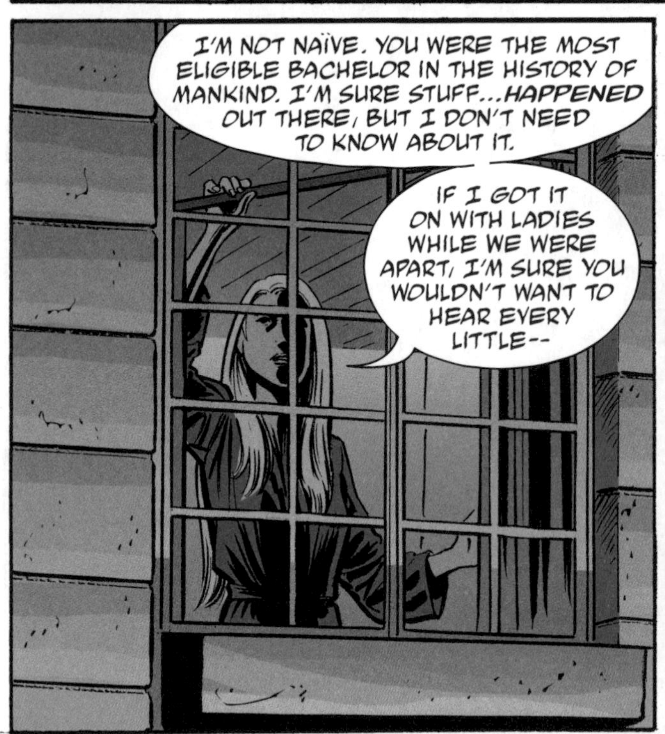
I'M NOT NAÏVE. YOU WERE THE MOST ELIGIBLE BACHELOR IN THE HISTORY OF MANKIND. I'M SURE STUFF...*HAPPENED* OUT THERE, BUT I DON'T NEED TO KNOW ABOUT IT.
IF I GOT IT ON WITH LADIES WHILE WE WERE APART, I'M SURE YOU WOULDN'T WANT TO HEAR EVERY LITTLE--

*YOU* WERE WITH *LADIES?!*

FUNNY BOY.
LOOK, ALL THAT MATTERS IS WE'RE TOGETHER. EVERYTHING ELSE IS JUST NOISE.
YOU AND I ARE NICK & NORA FROM HERE ON OUT, WHETHER YOU LIKE IT OR NOT.

IS...IS THIS STRANGE FOR YOU?

NO, MY TRIP HAS BEEN STRANGE. EVERYTHING ABOUT THIS IS COMPLETELY FAMILIAR.
I MEAN, YOU HAVEN'T AGED A SECOND, BETH.

YOU EVEN SMELL THE SAME.

AHUH

ARE YOU...ARE YOU CRYING? SERIOUSLY?
WHY THE HELL DO I ALWAYS DO THAT?
YOU KNEW.
YOU KNEW ALL ALONG.
THAT'S WHAT YOUR DREAMS WERE ABOUT.
YOU KNEW WHAT I WAS TRYING TO TELL YOU ON THE PHONE THAT DAY.
YOU KNEW I WAS GOING TO BREAK UP WITH YOU.

WHAT?

WE WERE MOVING IN DIFFERENT DIRECTIONS, YORICK.
I HAD A WHOLE WORLD TO EXPLORE AND YOU...YOU DIDN'T.

I CAN'T BREATHE.
YOU RECOGNIZED IT, TOO. IT'S WHY YOU BOUGHT THAT RING! WHY YOU FOUGHT SO HARD TO HANG ON TO ME.
I...I WASN'T SURE ABOUT IT MYSELF UNTIL I GOT TO AUSTRALIA. I NEVER WANTED TO HURT YOU, BUT I REALIZED--

ALL THIS WAY. ALL THIS TIME.
FOR A STUPID FUCKING PUNCHLINE.

NO! THINGS ARE DIFFERENT NOW!
WHY DO YOU THINK I'M GOING TO MARRY YOU!

SO YOU WOULD HAVE SAID NO TO THE MAN...
...BUT YES TO THE LAST MAN?

YOU KNOW IT'S NOT LIKE THAT!
YOU'RE NOT THE SAME PERSON YOU USED TO BE! YOU'VE CHANGED!

YOU HAVE ALWAYS BEEN AN EXTRAORDINARY HUMAN BEING, BUT I...I WASN'T SURE YOU WERE THE RIGHT PERSON FOR ME TO SPEND THE REST OF MY LIFE WITH.
BUT NOW, NOW YOU'RE COURAGEOUS AND STRONG AND...AND RESPONSIBLE. YOU'RE THE MAN I'VE BEEN DREAMING OF, LITERALLY.
THEN WHY WOULD YOU BRING UP DUMPING ME? JUST TO GET THE GUILT OFF YOUR CHEST?

I THOUGHT THE PAST WAS IMPORTANT TO YOU.

JESUS.
I JUST KEEP THINKING ABOUT THE SUMMER AFTER WE GRADUATED. PLAYING SCRABBLE AT YOUR MOM'S HOUSE ALL DAY, WATCHING MST3K ALL NIGHT.
YORICK...

I COULDN'T BELIEVE SOMEONE WAS SO INTERESTED IN ME.
BUT THAT WHOLE TIME, I WAS JUST A STRAIT-JACKET YOU WERE TRYING TO FIND YOUR WAY OUT OF.

WHATEVER, I NEED SOME AIR...
WAIT!
YOU CAN'T BE ALONE OUT THERE!

I HAVE SO MANY DIFFERENT WAYS TO RESPOND TO THAT, I DON'T EVEN KNOW WHERE TO BEGIN.

PLEASE DON'T LEAVE!
YORICK, I LOVE YOU!
I LOVE YOU, TOO, BETH.

SO FUCKING MUCH.

CREEEAK
YORICK?

BETH?
THANK CHRIST.

WHO THE HELL ARE...?

HERO?

IS MY BROTHER HERE?
WHAT? NO, HE...HE LEFT HOURS AGO. I'VE BEEN WAITING HERE ALL--
HERO, WE GOTTA CALL OFF THE HUNT.

CIBA AND NATALYA SPOTTED ISRAELIS A FEW BLOCKS FROM...
03

OH. MY GOD.
IT'S...IT'S REALLY HER, ISN'T IT?
WHAT IS GOING ON?

BETH, MEET BETH.
UM, HERO, THIS PROBABLY ISN'T THE TIME FOR--
AND THIS BEAUTIFUL LITTLE GIRL...

...IS YORICK'S DAUGHTER.

WHAT?

355

**Paris, France**
**Now**

YOU LOOK LIKE A LITTLE BALLERINA WHEN YOU PIROUETTE IN THAT THING.

YORICK?
HOW... HOW DID YOU FIND ME?
LEARNED FROM THE BEST.
JUST ABOUT GOT YOUR SKULL CRACKED OPEN BY HER, TOO.
WHAT ARE YOU DOING HERE, 'RICK? I THOUGHT YOU WERE SUPPOSED TO BE WITH BETH.
YEAH.
SO DID I.

WELL, THIS IS AWKWARD.

I'M SORRY, BETH, BUT BETH HAS A RIGHT TO KNOW ABOUT... BETH.
WHAT?
I KNOW, IT PROBABLY WOULD HAVE BEEN EASIER IF I'D NAMED HER BETTY OR ELIZABETH, BUT I'VE NEVER GOTTEN ALONG WITH CHICKS WHO GO BY THE VARIATIONS, HAVE YOU?

YORICK HAD A BABY?
WITH YOU?
LOOK, BEFORE THIS GETS ALL JERRY SPRINGER, YOU SHOULD KNOW NONE OF WHAT HAPPENED WAS YOUR BOYFRIEND'S--
AEEEE

AEEERR

EASY, AMPERSAND.
WE'RE ALL FRIENDS HERE.
YES.

WELL SAID.

HOLY SH--

--UNF!
AHH!

MS. BROWN, I PRESUME?
YOU HAVE YOUR BROTHER'S EYES.

AS DOES THIS LITTLE ONE.

WHO...?
YOU'RE... YOU'RE ALTER, RIGHT?
PLEASE. PLEASE DON'T HURT MY GIRL.

NOBODY IS GOING TO HURT ANYONE.
WHICH IS TO SAY THAT I HAVE NO INTENTION OF KILLING YOU PEOPLE.
UM, BITCH?

SO LONG AS YOU TELL ME WHERE TO FIND THE MAN OF THE HOUR.

FUCK.

FUCK, FUCK, FUCK.
DA.

NATALYA, IF YORICK'S NOT UP THERE, THOSE I.D.F. GOONS ARE GOING TO TORTURE OUR GIRLS TO DEATH. AND IF HE IS...
EITHER WAY, WE HAVE TO DO SOME-THING.

NYET.

BUT, I THOUGHT YOU'D TAKEN DOWN A BUNCH OF THESE ISRAELIS BEFORE?
THERE IS HUGE DIFFERENCES BETWEEN "BUNCH" AND ENTIRE HORSE-FUCKING *PLATOON*, CIBA.
AND LAST TIMES I BRING BATTLE, I WAS NOT ALSO PROTECTING ONLY SON OF RUSSIA.

THOSE WOMEN ARE OUR *SISTERS* NOW.
I'M NOT GOING TO LET VLAD GROW UP WITH THEIR BLOOD ON HIS HANDS.
WE HAVE NO LESS UGLY CHOICES.

IF YOU'RE JUST GOING TO RETREAT, THEN YOU MIGHT AS WELL TAKE MY BOY WITH YOU. GET...GET HIM SOMEWHERE SAFE. PLEASE. BUT LEAVE THE RIFLE WITH ME.
HELL, I...I DID A LITTLE HUNTING WITH MY GRANDFATHER. HOW MANY BULLETS ARE IN THAT THING, ANYWAY?

ENOUGH.

WHAT, YOU'RE GOING TO SHOOT ME?
I MAKE BEG OF YOU. NO MORE OF THIS BLUFFS. WE BOTH ARE KNOWING YOU WILL NOT LEAVE TINY VLADIMIR.
YOU ARE MOTHER. CHILD NEED YOU. I MUST TAKE YOU TOGETHER TO SAFETY ARMS OF MOSCOW.

I THOUGHT YOU WERE SUPPOSED TO BE SOME BIG BRAVE WAR HERO.
WHAT ABOUT THAT GODDAMN GOLD STAR YOU POLISH EVERY NIGHT?

<YOU KNOW WHAT THIS SHINY PIECE OF TIN IS, YOU FUCKING SPACE CADET?>
<IT'S THE WAY STUPID BOYS TRICK OTHER STUPID BOYS INTO DYING FOR BULLSHIT CAUSES...AND I'M DONE ACTING LIKE ONE OF THEM.>

I TOLD YOU.
I DON'T SPEAK RUSSIAN.

<YOU'LL LEARN.>

YOU FUCKED UP *ALREADY?*

IT'S NOT THAT SIMPLE. BETH AND I *BOTH* FUCKED UP.
I LOVE HER WITH ALL MY HEART, BUT WE...WE AREN'T MEANT FOR EACH OTHER. NOT ANYMORE.
YORICK, YOU KNEW THIS WAS GOING TO TAKE WORK. YOU CAN'T JUST RUN AWAY AT THE FIRST SIGN OF TROUBLE.

I'M NOT RUNNING *AWAY* FROM ANYTHING, 355.

WHAT DO YOU--
PLEASE.
I WANDERED THE ENTIRE CITY THINKING ABOUT THIS LAST NIGHT.

THERE'S SOMETHING I NEED TO TELL YOU.

DON'T.
I LOVE YOU, TOO, BUT THIS IS A MISTAKE.

...BUH?

WHAT ARE WE GONNA DO, SLEEP TOGETHER?
THE SECOND YOU CLIMB OFF ME, YOU'RE GOING TO REALIZE WHAT YOU'VE DONE AND GO RACING BACK TO BETH.
THAT'S JUST...YOU'RE WRONG.

FIRST OF ALL, I WOULDN'T BE ON TOP. I HAVE VERY POOR UPPER-BODY STRENGTH.
AND SECONDLY, I DON'T *WANT* TO SLEEP WITH YOU.

YOU DON'T?

NO!
I MEAN, YES! YES, I WOULD LOVE TO EVENTUALLY, MAYBE, SOMEDAY, YOU KNOW...DO THAT TO YOU.

I CAN'T BELIEVE YOU'RE NOT A VIRGIN.

ME NEITHER, AND I HAVE BETH TO THANK FOR THAT.
IT'D BE WRONG FOR ME TO START ANYTHING WITH YOU UNTIL I'M SURE THINGS ARE SETTLED WITH HER.
RIGHT. THAT'S...THAT'S THE RIGHT MOVE.

I'M A TERRIBLE PERSON, AREN'T I?
NO. NOT AT ALL. IT'S JUST...
IF YOU'RE THIS CONFUSED ABOUT THE WOMAN YOU JUST SPENT HALF A DECADE PINING FOR, HOW THE HELL CAN YOU BE SURE ABOUT ME?

DO YOU REMEMBER COLORADO?

YOUR SUICIDE INTERVENTION?
THAT'S ONE WAY OF PUTTING IT.

WHAT I SAW AT THE END...WHAT MADE ME REALIZE I DON'T WANT TO DIE, NO MATTER HOW MISERABLE LIFE GETS?
IT WAS YOU, AGENT 355.

IT WAS YOU.

OH.

AT THE TIME, I DIDN'T KNOW WHAT IT MEANT. I...
THAT'S NOT TRUE. I ALWAYS KNEW, I JUST DIDN'T *WANT* TO KNOW.
YOU LOST ME.

I KNEW I WANTED TO KEEP LIVING IN ANY WORLD THAT *YOU* WERE A PART OF.
BUT THAT WAS HARD TO ADMIT TO MYSELF...AND NOT JUST BECAUSE IT ENDED WITH A PREPOSITION.

FOR A MILLION WRONG REASONS, I NEEDED TO BELIEVE THAT *BETH* WAS WHY I KEPT PUTTING ONE FOOT IN FRONT OF THE OTHER.
BUT IT WASN'T WHO I WAS MARCHING *TOWARDS...* IT'S WHO WAS MARCHING NEXT TO ME EVERY STEP OF THE WAY.
"NEXT TO"? YOU WERE ALWAYS TEN PACES *BEHIND* MY BLACK ASS.

I'M SERIOUS, 355.
I AM, TOO, 'RICK.
BUT WHAT DO WE DO NOW...?

EAT A COCK!

TELL ME WHERE YORICK IS HIDING OR I REOPEN YOUR FRIEND'S *OLD WOUNDS.*
PERHAPS WHEN YOU PROVIDE US WITH ONE, HERO.

DON'T CUT HER!
I'LL TELL YOU WHAT I KNOW!
BETH, SHUT UP! SHE'LL *MURDER* MY BROTHER! SHE'LL--

HE WAS HERE LAST NIGHT, ALL RIGHT? BUT WE HAD A...A FIGHT. HE TOOK OFF.
AND WHERE DID HE ESCAPE TO AFTER YOUR LOVERS' QUARREL?
I HAVE NO IDEA. I *SWEAR.*

YES. YOU WILL...
‹LIEUTENANT-GENERAL!›

‹APOLOGIES FOR NOT REPORTING BACK SOONER, MA'AM. I GOT TRAPPED IN THE FROGS' USELESS SUBWAY SYSTEM WHILE I WAS--›
‹WHAT DO YOU HAVE, COLONEL?›

‹IT'S THE BLACK WOMAN, MA'AM. I FOUND HER.›
‹THE CULPER RING GIRL? WHERE?›
‹ACROSS TOWN. I FOLLOWED HER FROM A DRESS SHOP. SHE HAS A ROOM IN THE DES GRANDS HOMMES.›

‹FINE.›
‹WHO KNOWS IF MR. BROWN HAS PASSED ANY OF HIS TRICKS ONTO OUR HOSTAGES, SO YOU'LL STAND GUARD HERE WHILE THE REST OF THE TROOPS AND I CHECK YOUR HOTEL.›
I'M GONNA END YOU ASSHOLES!

‹YOU'RE TAKING EVERYONE?›
‹BUT MA'AM, THE CULPER AGENT'S ALL ALONE.›

‹WE'LL SEE.›

SO...
I KNOW.
I JUST DON'T WANT TO PULL A MOONLIGHTING AND SCREW UP WHAT WE HAVE GOING.

AND BEFORE YOU ASK, IT'S AN OLD P.I. SHOW WITH BRUCE WILLIS AND CYBILL SHEPHERD.
IT STARTED SUCKING AS SOON AS THEY STOPPED BEING ALL PLATONIC AT THE END OF SEASON THREE.
YOU WORRIED I'M GONNA CONFUSE YOU WITH BRUCE WILLIS?

FUCK THAT, THREE-FIFTY.
I'M CYBILL, *YOU'RE* BRUCE.

YOU CAN KNOCK OFF THE WHOLE *"THREE-FIFTY"* THING, YOU KNOW.

BUT YOU ALWAYS SAID--
THAT'S OVER NOW.
YOU'RE THE ONE WHO TOLD ME I DIDN'T HAVE TO BE A NUMBER ANYMORE, RIGHT?
THEN... WHAT AM I SUPPOSED TO CALL YOU?
HOW 'BOUT THE NAME MY PARENTS GAVE ME?
I THOUGHT THAT PERSON DIED WITH YOUR FAMILY.
YEAH.
SO DID I.

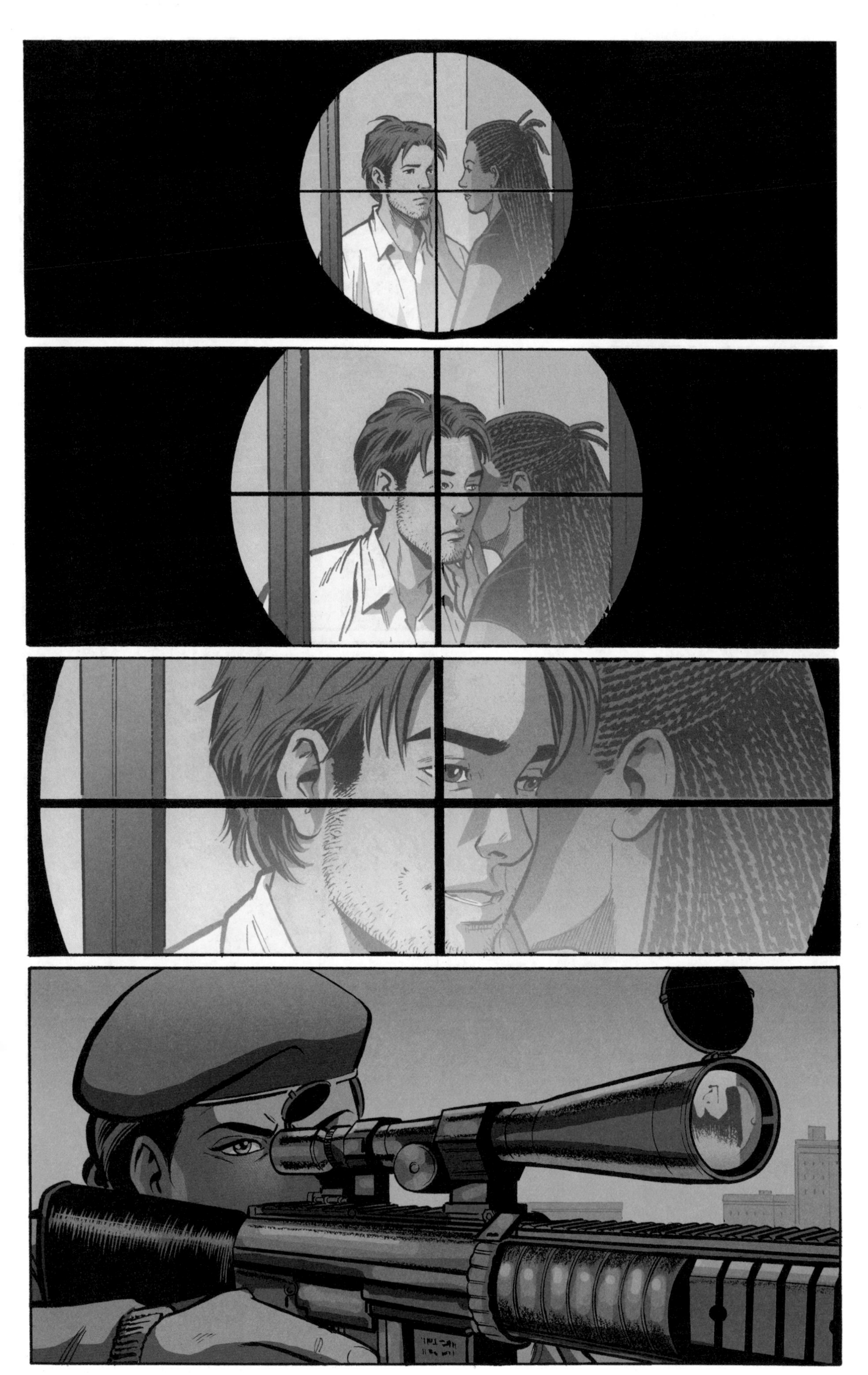

WOW, THAT'S A DISAPPOINTMENT.

LIKE IT'S ANY MORE RIDICULOUS THAN YOUR NAME?

I'M JOKING, DUMMY.
IT'S PERFECT. IT'S REALLY--
KRACK

WHAT... WHAT WAS THAT?

**Paris, France**
**Now**

HOW THE HELL DID YORICK PISS OFF THE **ENTIRE** NATION OF ISRAEL?
HIS *MERCHANT OF VENICE* THESIS?
JUST SHUT UP AND LET ME THINK, BETH. BOTH OF YOU.

I NEVER WANTED TO BE A SOLDIER. OR MUCH OF ANYTHING, REALLY.
WHAT'S YOUR EUPHEMISM? ***HOMEMAKER?*** WHY WASN'T IT ENOUGH FOR YOU PEOPLE TO JUST BE A MOTHER?

<I PROMISE I WILL BE A GOOD MOTHER TO YOU.>
HERO, ***PLEASE!***
THIS BITCH IS GONNA KIDNAP BETH JUNIOR!

THE COLONEL ISN'T THAT STUPID, IS SHE?
SHE KNOWS HER BOSS WILL HUNT HER TO THE ENDS OF THE EARTH IF...IF SHE COMES BACK AND FINDS THE WOMAN SHE LEFT ON GUARD HAS ***ABANDONED*** HER POST.

ALTER HAS LOST HER MIND.
SHE WOULD NOT CARE IF I EXECUTED ALL THREE OF YOU.

THEN DO IT, YOU **FUCKING VIRGIN!**
KILL ME AND STEAL MY BABY, SEE IF THAT WILL MAKE YOU FEEL LIKE LESS OF A BARREN PIECE OF DRIED SHIT.

CAREFUL, WOMAN.
OR I WILL TAKE MORE THAN JUST YOUR--
'SUKA!

'TCHYO ZA GA'LIMA?!
I'M GUESSING THAT'S RUSSIAN FOR "MINE'S BIGGER THAN YOURS."

NATALYA!
ALWAYS WITH THE LAST-MINUTE HAN SOLO.

INCORRECT, OUTER-SPACE CADET. IT WAS OUR FAVORITE SISTER OF NASA WHO GUILT ME INTO PUTTING MY TITS ON LINE TO RESCUING YOU HELPLESS ORNAMENTS.
NOW THEN, UNHAND CHILD OR I UNHEAD YOU.

WAIT, WHAT?
CIBA WEBER, LOVELY TO MEET YOU.
CIBA WEBER--THE ASTRONAUT?

OOH, I LIKE THIS ONE ALREADY.
YOU HAVE A SON? IS HE...?
NOT YOUR BOYFRIEND'S. YOU ARE YORICK'S FAIRY PRINCESS, RIGHT? COME ON...

...LET'S GET YOU YOUR HAPPY ENDING.

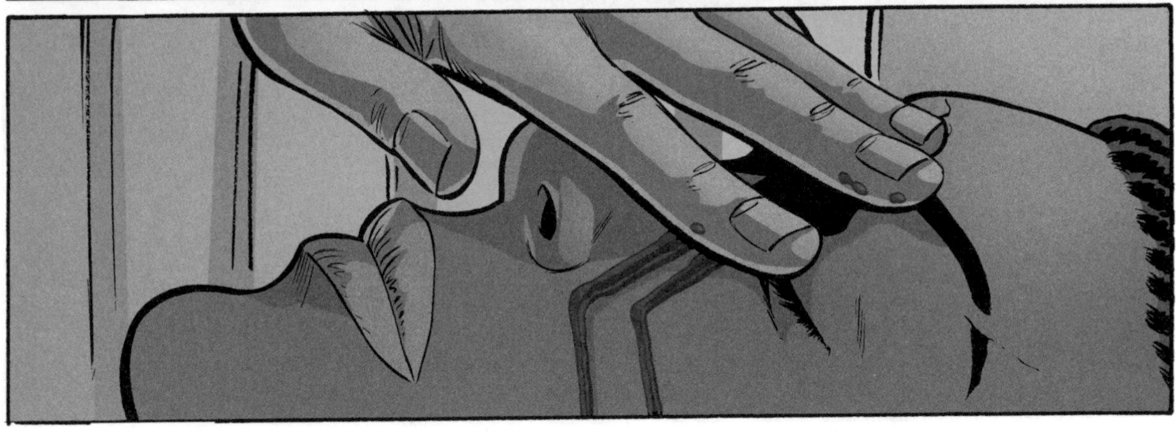

KERRASH

TSSSSSSSS

⟨IT'S DONE, LIEUTENANT-GENERAL.⟩

⟨THE ENTIRE HOTEL HAS BEEN GASSED. ANYONE YOU LEFT ALIVE IN THERE IS FAST ASLEEP NOW.⟩
⟨GIVE IT ANOTHER THIRTY SECONDS TO DISSIPATE AND WE'LL STORM THE BUILDING.⟩
⟨YOU'LL DO NO SUCH THING, SERGEANT. I'M GOING IN *ALONE.*⟩

⟨MA'AM?⟩
⟨BUT THE LAST MALE...⟩
⟨YOU KNOW YOUR ORDER AND WHAT WILL HAPPEN IF YOU DISOBEY IT.⟩

⟨I NEED A LITTLE PRIVACY.⟩

SO.
NOT WITH A BANG, BUT A--

AH!

THINK

UHN!

KRACK

HKK.

WHUMMP
RAAA!

KASSH

HAA!

KEESSHH

NOT...SO TOUGH... WITHOUT YOUR LITTLE PHALLUS, EH?
I GUESS MS. 355 DIDN'T TEACH YOU ENOUGH TO...

DAMN.
YOU'RE THE ONE WHO SHOT HER, AREN'T YOU?
OF COURSE. I HAD TO.

WHY?
BECAUSE 355 CAUSED IT.
CAUSED WHAT?

THE DEATH OF ALL THE MEN.

GET AWAY FROM HER.
IT WAS HER BOSSES IN THE CULPER RING WHO STARTED IT, BUT YOUR "FRIEND" DID HER BEST TO COVER UP THEIR DIRTY WORK.
WHY DO YOU THINK SHE WAS FOLLOWING YOU AROUND THE PLANET? TO MAKE SURE YOU DIDN'T GET TOO CLOSE TO THE TRUTH.

NO.
SHE AND I FOUND THE CAUSE OF THE PLAGUE TOGETHER.

CONVENIENT. BUT THE DOCUMENTS I DECLASSIFIED IN TEL AVIV SUGGEST THAT THE CULPERS WERE LOOKING FOR WAYS TO DEAL WITH THE EMERGING THREAT OF CHINA.
THEY RELEASED A CHEMICAL AGENT IN BEIJING THAT WAS SUPPOSED TO PREVENT ITS WOMEN FROM CONCEIVING MALE CHILDREN, AND THUS CRIPPLE THE CHINESE ECONOMY WITHIN A GENERATION. BUT SOMETHING CLEARLY WENT--

KA-CLICK

YOU LIE FOR SHIT.
WHAT ARE YOU AFTER? REALLY?

I CAN SEE IT IN YOUR EYES. YOU'VE KILLED A WOMAN SINCE LAST WE MET, HAVEN'T YOU?
YOU'RE NOT ALONE.
I KILLED YOUR MOTHER.

WHAT?

SHE BETRAYED ME, SO I SHOT HER MYSELF.
THERE'S AN OBITUARY OR TWO IN MY POCKET IF YOU DON'T BELIEVE *THAT*...BUT YOU DO, DON'T YOU? BELIEVE THAT I MURDERED YOUR MOM. YOUR **MOMMY**.

WHY... WHY ARE YOU TELLING ME THIS?

OH MY GOD.

WHAT? WHAT ARE YOU WAITING FOR? I SPIT ON YOUR MOTHER'S *CORPSE*. I PUT A BULLET IN THE BLACK BRAIN OF YOUR TAGALONG *WHORE*. I--
THAT'S WHAT THIS HAS BEEN ABOUT.
THE WHOLE TIME.

YOU'VE BEEN TRYING TO COMMIT SUICIDE, TOO.

THIS ISN'T SUICIDE.
THIS IS WAR.

AFTER EVERYTHING I'VE BEEN THROUGH? EVERYTHING I SACRIFICED? I HAVE A RIGHT TO DIE IN BATTLE!
AND NOT AT THE HANDS OF...OF SOME GIRL!

IT HAS TO BE YOU, GODDAMMIT! FUCKING FIGHT ME!
WHY WON'T YOU ACT LIKE WHAT YOU ARE?

WHY?

⟨WE'RE GOING IN.⟩

⟨I DON'T CARE WHAT SHE SAID, I DIDN'T COME THIS FAR TO--⟩
⟨SERGEANT!⟩

⟨IT'S HIM.⟩

WHAT NOW, MR. BROWN?
HAVE YOU COME TO GIVE MY TROOPS ONE OF YOUR SELF-RIGHTEOUS *LECTURES?*

NO...YOU WANT TO KILL ME IN *FRONT* OF THEM, DON'T YOU?
THEN GET ON WITH IT.

<MY NAME IS NOT ALTER, IT'S *YEDIDA,* SISTER OF RACHEL.>
<AND I AM FINISHED... FINISHED RUNNING FROM THE ANGEL OF DEATH!>

*<DO YOU HEAR ME?>*

THWOCK

ENOUGH.

EEND

I TOLD YOU TO STAY WITH THE MOMS AND THE KIDS, BETH.
AND I TOLD YOU I'M NEITHER, HERO.
BESIDES, THIS IS ALL MY FAULT. YORICK NEVER WOULD HAVE LEFT IF I HAD JUST--

HUSHED.

JESUS CHRIST.
IS THAT...?

YOU'RE ALIVE!
BUT THE ISRAELIS...?
GONE.

355?

OH.

OH, MAN.

60

UM.
HEY.

HOLY SHIT.
YOU'RE...YOU'RE HIM, AREN'T YOU?

I GUESS SO.
AND YOU MUST BE CATHERINE.
JESUS, MY BOSSES AT THE CULPER SPHERE TOLD ME THIS WAS AN IMPORTANT GIG, BUT I HAD NO IDEA IT WAS YOU, UH...SIRE?

NO, WAIT. "SIR." SIR, RIGHT?
I'VE NEVER ACTUALLY USED THAT WORD BEFORE.

WELL, DO ME A FAVOR AND NEVER USE IT AGAIN.
ROGER THAT.
APOLOGIES FOR BEING SUCH A FUCKIN' FRITZ. THIS IS JUST... STRANGE.

WHAT, YOU'VE NEVER MET A CLONE BEFORE?

UH, PRETTY MUCH EVERYONE OUR AGE WAS CLONED FROM SOMEBODY, RIGHT?

NO, I KNOW. THAT'S THE JOKE.
WOMEN SOMETIMES FREAK OUT BECAUSE I'M USUALLY THE FIRST GUY THEY'VE EVER SEEN IN PERSON, SO I ALWAYS SAY...

...SORRY.
HUMOR ISN'T MY STRONG SUIT.
ANYWAY, THE PRESIDENT IS WAITING FOR YOU.

MIGHT AS WELL GET THIS OVER WITH, HUH?

## Paris, France
## Sixty Years from Now

23PF

BETH?

WE HAVE A SITUATION, I'M AFRAID.
ANOTHER INDIA-PAKISTAN PISSING MATCH?
NO, THIS IS MORE OF A GOOD NEWS/BAD NEWS THING.

IRAN HAS THE BOMB.

EXCUSE ME?
THE ONE SATELLITE WE'VE GOT LEFT CONFIRMS IT.
AND HOW THE HELL IS THAT GOOD NEWS?

WELL, I'D SAY PRODUCING TWENTY-FIVE KILOGRAMS OF HIGHLY ENRICHED URANIUM IS A SIGNIFICANT BREAKTHROUGH...
...ESPECIALLY FOR A SOCIETY WHERE WOMEN WEREN'T EVEN ALLOWED TO **SING IN PUBLIC** BEFORE LE GRAND DÉPART STRUCK.

THE BAD NEWS, OF COURSE...
YES, "MEET THE NEW BOSS."
WE'RE GOING TO NEED THE RUSSIANS' HELP TO DEFUSE THE SITUATION. I HAVE TO TALK WITH **VLADIMIR.**

THE CZAR? BETH, HE'S NOT EXACTLY ON SPEAKING TERMS WITH THE NORTH ATLANTIC SORORITÉ THESE DAYS.
THEN WE'LL COMMUNICATE THROUGH BACK CHANNELS. HIS MOTHER USED TO HELP CHANGE MY DIAPERS FOR GOD'S SAKE.
BUT CIBA WEBER DIED YEARS AGO.

AND REMEMBER THE OLD RUSSIAN WOMAN I INTRODUCED YOU TO AT HER FUNERAL? SHE STILL HAS VLAD'S EAR. WE'LL SEND A COMMUNIQUÉ THROUGH HER.
NATALYA, RIGHT? HER ENGLISH WAS EXCELLENT.
HEH.
WHAT?

LONG STORY.
MADEMOISELLE LA PRÉSIDENTE?

EXCUSEZ-MOI.
EST-CE QUE JE PEUX ME PRÉSENTER--

IT'S ALL RIGHT, CATHERINE.
I APPARENTLY POSSESS JUST ENOUGH "QUALITY OF FRENCHMAN" THAT MY COUNTRYWOMEN AREN'T THREATENED WHEN I FLIRT WITH MY NATIVE TONGUE.

CHRIST, WILL YOU LOOK AT THOSE EYEBROWS?
THEY WERE RIGHT ABOUT THIS ONE. IT'S LIKE YOU'RE REALLY HIM.
THANK YOU, MA'AM, BUT TECHNICALLY, I'M JUST LOWLY YORICK BROWN THE SEVENTEENTH.

YES, I'M WELL AWARE OF THE BURDENS OF CARRYING ANOTHER'S NAME.

MY SURROGATE GAVE ME ONE OF YOUR MOM'S BOOKS ON SECULAR HUMANISM.
IT WAS REALLY... INTERESTING.

NICE OF YOU TO SAY, BUT BETH SENIOR CONVERTED BACK TO POST-VATICAN III CATHOLICISM LATE IN LIFE.
ATHEISM APPARENTLY LOSES ITS LUSTER WHEN THE FINISH LINE APPROACHES.

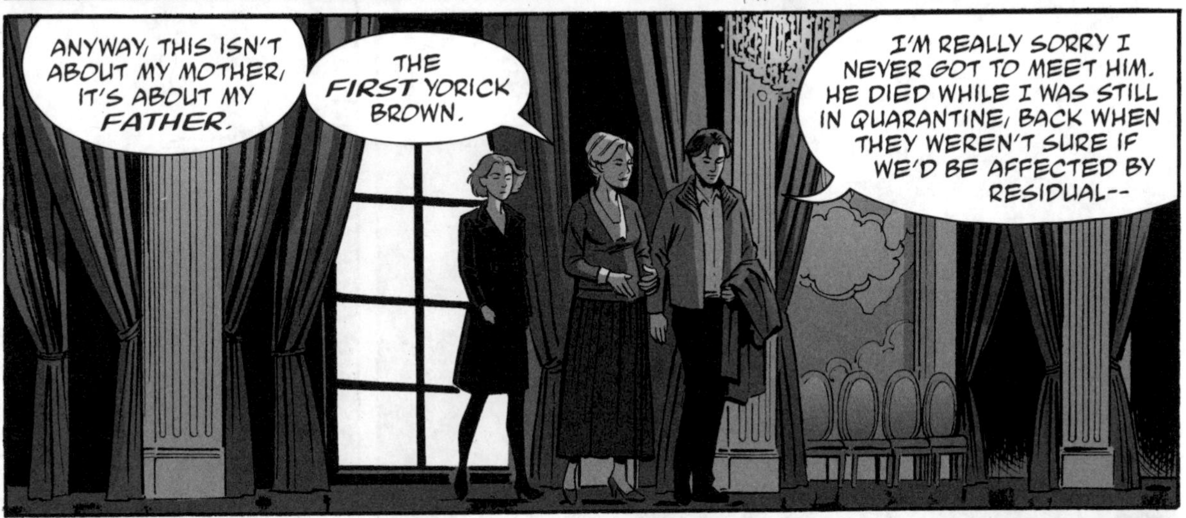
ANYWAY, THIS ISN'T ABOUT MY MOTHER, IT'S ABOUT MY FATHER.
THE FIRST YORICK BROWN.
I'M REALLY SORRY I NEVER GOT TO MEET HIM. HE DIED WHILE I WAS STILL IN QUARANTINE, BACK WHEN THEY WEREN'T SURE IF WE'D BE AFFECTED BY RESIDUAL--

THAT'S THE THING, YORICK.
MY DAD IS STILL ALIVE.

HUH?

HE WAS A WONDERFUL FATHER, BUT HIS RELATIONSHIP WITH MY MOM WAS...COMPLICATED.
EVEN FROM AN EARLY AGE, I KNEW THEY WERE REALLY ONLY STAYING TOGETHER FOR ME.

NO MATTER HOW WELL HE TRIED TO HIDE IT, IT WAS CLEAR DAD WAS ALWAYS IN LOVE WITH SOMEONE ELSE.
THE OTHER BETH, RIGHT?
BETH DEVILLE?

THAT'S WHAT THE SHITTY BIOPIC WOULD HAVE YOU BELIEVE...BUT THERE WAS ACTUALLY ANOTHER WOMAN.
I DON'T THINK HE WAS EVER THE SAME AFTER HE LOST HER, AND TIME ONLY SEEMED TO MAKE THE PAIN WORSE.

ON HIS MOST RECENT BIRTHDAY, DAD TRIED TO KILL HIMSELF.

WITH ALL THE THREATS HE'D BEEN RECEIVING FROM THE DAUGHTERS OF THE REVOLUTION, WE DECIDED TO SPIN HIS HOSPITALIZATION AS "DEATH BY NATURAL CAUSES."
HE'S BEEN SECRETLY COMMITTED HERE AT THE PALAIS DE L'ÉLYSEE EVER SINCE.
WHAT DO YOU MEAN *COMMITTED?*

YORICK, MY DAD WASN'T ALWAYS A MELANCHOLY MAN.
HE DOESN'T HAVE MUCH LONGER, AND I'D LIKE FOR HIM TO LAUGH JUST ONCE MORE BEFORE HE GOES.

I HAVE REASON TO BELIEVE YOU'RE JUST THE MAN FOR THAT JOB.
ME?
YEAH, BUT... NO.

TRUST ME, JUST SEEING YOU IS GOING TO REMIND HIM OF HAPPIER TIMES.
ALL YOU HAVE TO DO IS BE YOURSELF.

WHAM

HN.

DID YOU KNOW ELVIS HAD A TWIN BROTHER?

WHO'S ELVIS?

HE WAS A *REAL*...
GUY WHO COULD MAKE WOMEN FAINT JUST BY SHAKING HIS HIPS.

FORGET IT. THEIR TURN AT THE MICROPHONE NOW.
SO, YOU'RE MY GHOST OF CHRISTMAS PAST, HUH?
UM, ACTUALLY, IT'S JULY. AND I'M NOT A GHOST, I'M YOUR GENETIC--

I'M *OLD*, KID, NOT RETARDED.

OH.
I SUPPOSE MY OVER-PROTECTIVE BABY GIRL TOLD YOU I TRIED TO OFF MYSELF.
WELL, THAT'S BULLSHIT. IT WAS JUST A... A *JOKE*. BECAUSE I WAS EIGHTY-FIVE AND ABOUT TO BE EIGHTY-SIXED. LIKE THE TURN OF PHRASE?

SOUNDS HILARIOUS.

WHAT'S YOUR STORY, JUNIOR?
MY STORY?
ANOTHER BORING BILDUNGSROMAN, PROBABLY. YOU HAVE A LADY FRIEND OR WHAT?
NOT YET. I HAVEN'T BEEN A FREE MAN FOR THAT LONG. BUT I'M TRYING.

IT'S LIKE THAT OLD SAYING.
WE SPEND NINE MONTHS TRYING TO GET OUT OF A WOMAN AND THE REST OF OUR LIVES TRYING TO GET BACK IN.
DO YOURSELF A SPECTACULAR FAVOR AND STOW THAT FRAT-BOY HORSECRAP WITH A QUICKNESS.
GIRLS AREN'T A GAME.

NOT ONE THAT YOU CAN WIN.

HELLO?

I CAN HEAR YOU, BITCH.
GET YOUR POACHING ASS OUT HERE BEFORE I BLOW IT OFF.

EASY, HERO.

YORICK?
EEK

WHAT HAPPENED TO YOU?
THANKS, YOU LOOK GOOD, TOO.
YOU KNOW WHAT I MEAN. I THOUGHT YOU WERE TRYING TO ENJOY WEDDED BLISS WITH OTHER BETH. WHAT THE HELL ARE YOU DOING IN THE KALAHARI? 'CAUSE IF YOU'RE LOOKING FOR CLOSURE...

NO, STOPPED LOOKING FOR THAT A LONG TIME AGO.
JUST WANTED TO BRING SOMETHING I FORGOT TO GIVE YOU AT MOM'S CEREMONY.

WHAT IS IT?
SOMETHING I GOT FROM A FRIEND OF MINE.
FIGURED YOU'D BE LESS LIKELY TO SHOOT YOUR EYE OUT WITH IT WHILE YOU'RE OUT HERE DOING YOUR WHOLE "WHITE WOMAN'S BURDEN" THING.
THINK

THANKS, BUT IT'S NOT LIKE THAT.
THE LAST OF THE LIONESSES NEED OUR PROTECTION, BUT THESE WOMEN DON'T NEED A GODDAMN THING.

EVERYONE THOUGHT OF THE "BUSHMEN" AS PRIMITIVE, BUT THEY TREATED THEIR WIVES AND DAUGHTERS AS EQUALS ABOUT 20,000 YEARS BEFORE THE REST OF THE PLANET EVEN CONSIDERED THE IDEA.

WHEN ALL THE BOYS DIED, THE SAN WOMEN JUST DIVIDED THE HUNTING AND GATHERING DUTIES AMONG THEMSELVES.

THEY DID WHAT WE ALL DID, REALLY. THEY ADAPTED. THEY EVOLVED.
THEY MOVED ON.

WOW, YOU'RE EVEN STARTING TO SOUND LIKE HER.

SORRY.
SHE'LL ACTUALLY BE BACK SOON IF YOU WANT TO--
THANKS, BUT AMPERSAND AND I SHOULD PROBABLY HIT THE ROAD. WE HAVE A LOT TO DO, AND I WANT TO BE BACK FOR MY LITTLE ONE'S EIGHTH BIRTHDAY PARTY.

WHERE ARE YOU GENTLEMEN OFF TO NEXT?
WALES, BELIEVE IT OR NOT. I'M TAKING A MONTH OFF TO DO A LITTLE RESEARCH FOR MY FIRST NOVEL.
SERIOUSLY? WHAT'S IT ABOUT?

I DON'T KNOW YET. BUT THERE'S THIS OLD WELSH CUSTOM I READ ABOUT. THE MELLTITH, THEY CALLED IT. THOUGHT IT MIGHT MAKE FOR GOOD HISTORICAL FICTION.
APPARENTLY, WEDDING PARTIES WOULD CHOP DOWN TREES AND START FIRES AND COME UP WITH ALL SORTS OF CRAZY OBSTACLES TO STOP THE GROOM FROM GETTING TO HIS BRIDE ON THE BIG DAY. IT WAS SUPPOSED TO PROVE A MAN'S WORTH, I GUESS.

YOU STILL THINK THAT'S WHAT IT WAS ALL ABOUT, HUH?
HOW DO YOU MEAN?
HERO?

COOL, HERE SHE COMES.
BE NICE FOR YOU TWO TO AT LEAST SAY...

...HELLO?
YOU ALL RIGHT?

I THOUGHT THAT HOMEOPATHIC STUFF I FOUND WAS HELPING WITH YOUR VOICES.
JUST SINGING TO MYSELF, BETH.
WHEW. EXCITED ABOUT DINNER?
I BELIEVE TEAM DEVILLE/BROWN IS CLOSING IN ON THE RECORD FOR MOST MONGONGO NUTS EVER CONSUMED BY TWO--
HASN'T ANYONE EVER TOLD YOU THAT WOMEN SHOULD BE SEEN AND NOT HEARD?
I THOUGHT THAT WAS CHILDREN.
WHATEVER, COME HERE, BEAUTIFUL...

SO, YOU MOVING HERE OR WHAT?
TO GAY PAREE?
NO, I'M THINKING ABOUT RELOCATING TO CANADA. I'M INTERESTED IN LAW, AND ONE OF MY BROTHERS TOLD ME THE UNIVERSITY OF OTTAWA MIGHT BE OPEN TO ENROLLING A MALE STUDENT.

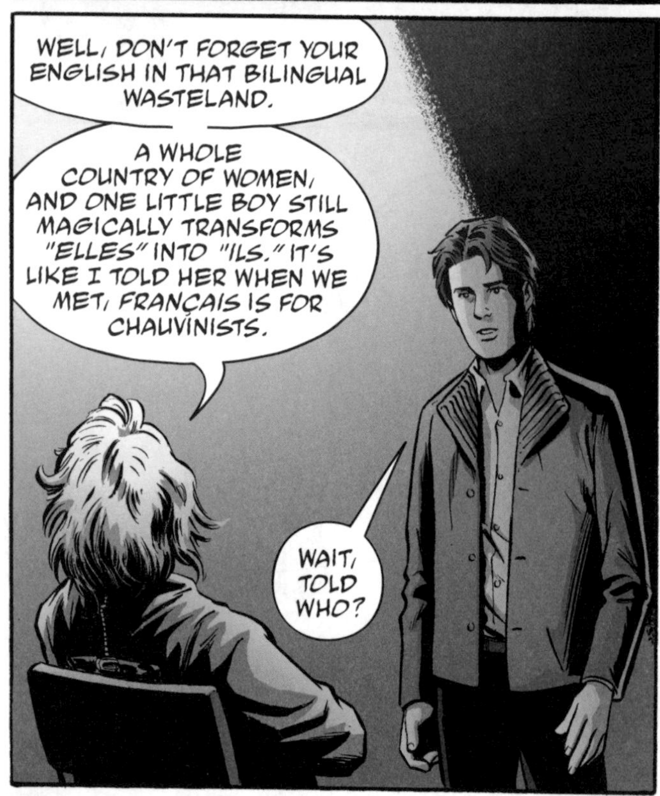
WELL, DON'T FORGET YOUR ENGLISH IN THAT BILINGUAL WASTELAND.
A WHOLE COUNTRY OF WOMEN, AND ONE LITTLE BOY STILL MAGICALLY TRANSFORMS "ELLES" INTO "ILS." IT'S LIKE I TOLD HER WHEN WE MET, FRANÇAIS IS FOR CHAUVINISTS.
WAIT, TOLD WHO?

IT DOESN'T REALLY--
HKK KOFF KOFF KOFF HKK

HOLD ON.
I'LL...I'LL GET YOU SOME FRESH AIR.

HHH.

YOU SAID YOU HAD BROTHERS.
THE REST OF THEM ALL LIKE YOU? LIKE US?
DNA-WISE, YOU MEAN? NO, THEY FINALLY STARTED ENGINEERING NEW STRAINS LAST YEAR.

"NEW STRAINS."
LIKE A DISEASE.

ABOUT RIGHT.

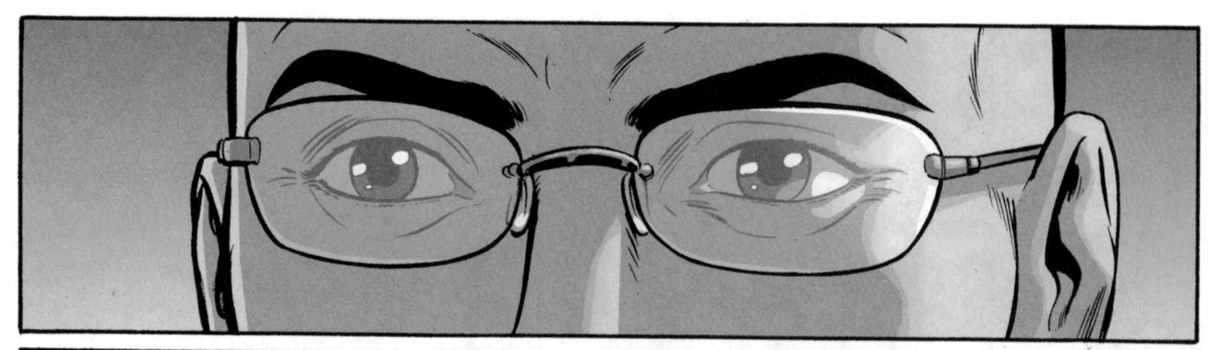

DOC?

DR. MANN?
DONT ERASE

DON'T MAKE ME SAY "ALLISON."
I STILL CAN'T BRING MYSELF TO CALL YOU--
HELLO, FOUR EYES.

THANKS FOR COMING, MATE.
OH, NO.
AM... AM I TOO LATE?
I'M SORRY, ROSE.
I'M SO SORRY.
SHE TRIED TO HOLD ON FOR YOU...FOR *BOTH* OF YOU.

SO THIS IS REALLY...?
THE FIRST OF MANY, HOPEFULLY.
TOOK HER AGES TO MAKE A COPY OF YOU THAT AMPERSAND'S BROOD WOULD INOCULATE INSTEAD OF ANNIHILATE, BUT I THINK WE HAVE A WINNER.
URN
BUT HOW ARE *YOU*?
I'M...I'LL FIND A WAY TO SOLDIER ON.
AND EVEN IF I DON'T, SOMEONE ELSE WILL CARRY HER TORCH.
NO WORRIES THERE.

"DR. MEN."
THEY'RE YOUNG, BUT SMART.
THE ELDEST ALREADY HELPED THE HARTLE TWINS SOLVE THE LIVESTOCK CRISIS BACK IN THE STATES.

THEY ALL TALK WITH THEIR HANDS JUST LIKE SHE DID.
IT'S... IT'S KIND OF BEAUTIFUL.

WHICH REMINDS ME.
SHE WANTED YOU TO SEE THIS.
A LOCK OF HAIR? DON'T TELL ME SHE CURED *BALDNESS* ON THE WAY OUT, TOO.

YORICK.
SHE TOOK IT OFF AGENT 355.

MOLECULAR GENETICS
HUMAN GENETICS
GENOMIC DIVERSITY
MAPPING
EPIDEMIOLOGY
PROGRAMMING
HISTORY OF GENETICS
WHAT?

ALI ALWAYS KNEW HOW MUCH SHE MEANT TO YOU.
AND EVER SINCE WE STARTED CLONING FEMALES EN MASSE, WE'VE HAVE THE WHEREWITHAL TO "BRING BACK," FOR LACK OF A BETTER PHRASE, ANY WOMAN, LIVING OR--
NO.

THANK YOU, BUT NO.
I...I WOULDN'T WANT THAT.
NO OFFENSE, LUV, BUT IT'S NOT ALL ABOUT YOU. WHAT IF THREE-FIFTY WANTED TO...

RIGHT THEN.

SAY NO MORE.

AHK

TOOK 'EM LONG ENOUGH.

TO START MAKING OTHER GUYS, YOU MEAN? WELL, THEY'VE HAD TROUBLE WITH THE Y-CHROMOSOME, APPARENTLY.
THAT'S BECAUSE CLONING IS *CRAP*.
YOU CAN PHOTOCOPY MANN'S BRAIN AS MANY TIMES AS YOU WANT, BUT WITHOUT HER ASSHOLE DAD PUSHING THOSE GIRLS EVERY STEP OF THE WAY, YOU'LL NEVER HAVE HER *MIND*.

TO BE HONEST, RIGHT ABOUT NOW, I'M REALLY THANKFUL FOR THE WHOLE NATURE-NURTURE DIVIDE.

THAT A BOY.

WHOA.
THESE LITTLE GUYS ARE SO WELL-BEHAVED.

TELL ME ABOUT IT.
A HUNDRED MONKEYS LATER AND THEY STILL HAVEN'T GOTTEN HIM RIGHT.

SORRY?
YEAH.
ME, TOO.

DON'T WORRY, BUDDY.
EVERY-THING'S GOING TO BE OKAY.
CFF

I KNOW IT'S HARD, BUT IT WON'T BE MUCH LONGER, AMPERSAND.
WE'RE GOING TO VISIT AN OLD FRIEND. YOU ALWAYS LIKED HER, REMEMBER?

FFF

YOU HUNGRY?
OKAY, PAL, HERE WE GO.

COME ON, DUMMY.
YOU LOVE GRAPES.
TK

PLEASE EAT.

THANKS.

REMEMBER BRAZIL?
WHEN THOSE ROLLER DERBY PSYCHOS HAD ME TIED UP, AND YOU STARTED SCREAMING AT THE TOP OF YOUR LUNGS WHEN I TRIED TO GET OUT?

YOU HAVE BEEN ONE PIECE OF SHIT PET.

TSSS

AH, FUCK.

WHY THE FUCK DID I DO THAT?

THEY SAID IT WOULDN'T HURT, AMP. I...I DIDN'T WANT YOU TO HURT ANYMORE.
THEY PROMISED IT WOULD BE QUICK.

YEAH.
I KNOW.

I KNOW.

355
PEACE

SO THIS IS IT, HUH?
WHAT'S THAT?
YOU KNOW, GROWING OLD. ALL I HAVE TO LOOK FORWARD TO IS PAIN AND MISERY AND...AND HEARTBREAK.

NO.
NO, FIRST COMES BOYHOOD. YOU GET TO PLAY WITH SOLDIERS AND SPACEMEN, COW-BOYS AND NINJAS, PIRATES AND ROBOTS.
BUT BEFORE YOU KNOW IT, ALL THAT COMES TO AN END.

AND THEN, REMO WILLIAMS, IS WHEN THE ADVENTURE BEGINS.

I HAVE NO IDEA WHAT YOU'RE TALKING ABOUT.
MY LIFE HAS BEEN A TOTAL WASTE SO FAR, AND I'M ALREADY AN ADULT!

...
HOW OLD ARE YOU?

TWENTY-TWO.

HEH.

WHAT?

I TURNED YOUR AGE A FEW WEEKS BEFORE THE PLAGUE HIT, BACK WHEN MY LIFE WAS EVEN MORE OF A MESS THAN IT IS NOW.
I WAS JOBLESS, BEHIND ON RENT, MY GIRL WAS GONE...
UM, ARE YOUR MONKEYS OKAY?

AND MY OLD MAN WRITES ME THIS BIRTHDAY NOTE THAT SAYS:
"A PAIR OF DEUCES AIN'T MUCH...BUT SOMETIMES, IT CAN BE A WINNING HAND."

ARE... ARE THEY SUPPOSED TO BE DOING THIS?

YOU'LL BE FINE, 'RICK.
JUST GO OUT THERE AND GET YOUR HEART BROKEN IN, SO IT'LL BE READY WHEN YOU REALLY NEED IT.

HEY!
CALL THEM OFF, WOULD YOU?! THEY'RE GONNA CLAW THE EYES RIGHT OUT OF MY...

YORICK?

NO.

NO!

OUCH!

I THOUGHT YOU WERE SUPPOSED TO BE A DOCTOR!

I AM, UNLESS MY BOARD CERTIFICATION EXPIRED WITH THE BOARD.
WHATEVER, JUST START DOING NO HARM ALREADY!
WHY DID YOU RUN BAREFOOT INTO A DEBRIS FIELD ANYWAY?

BECAUSE I THOUGHT THERE'D BE PEANUTS, NOT A SEA OF RUSTY NAILS!
AND NOW I'VE PROBABLY GOT LOCKJAW!
WE SHOULD BE SO LUCKY.

YOU WON'T BE LAUGHING WHEN I CATCH UP WITH THE REST OF THESE GUYS.
I'M OFF TO LOOK FOR A FIRST-AID KIT.
DON'T PUT ANY PRESSURE ON THAT THING.

GLRT
FUCKIN' A.
HEY.

YOU OKAY?

NO THANKS TO YOU.
I THOUGHT YOU WERE SUPPOSED TO BE MY GUARDIAN ANGEL.
WHERE THE HELL HAVE YOU BEEN?

GETTING YOU THESE.
PEANUTS

AH.
UH-HUH.

DO YOU BELIEVE IN HEAVEN?

JESUS, YOU'RE NOT GONNA *DIE*.
MAYBE, MAYBE NOT.
I'M JUST CURIOUS.

LIKE, DO I THINK THERE'S LIFE AFTER DEATH?
I HOPE NOT.
BUT, DIDN'T YOU SAY ALL OF YOUR FAMILY IS DEAD? WOULDN'T YOU WANT TO SEE THEM AGAIN?

YEAH, THAT'D BE NICE. FOR A WHILE. BUT THEN...
NAH, I HOPE THIS IS THE END OF THE LINE.
WHY?

WHY NOT?

OKAY, THINK OF A CARD, BUT DON'T TELL ME WHAT IT IS YET.

YOU ARE A STRANGE KID.

GOT IT?
IT'S THE QUEEN OF HEARTS, RIGHT?

NOT EVEN CLOSE.
SIX OF CLUBS.
SERIOUSLY? DAMN. EVERY WOMAN I'VE EVER MET HAS SAID QUEEN OF HEARTS.

YOU MAY NEED TO MEET MORE WOMEN.

HA HA.

WHAT?

I'M SORRY, MA'AM.
I...I ONLY TOOK MY EYES OFF HIM FOR A SECOND.

HE JUMPED?

NO.

HE ESCAPED.

POIRE €7.50
ÉCROUS

# Alas

Brian K. Vaughan
WRITER

Pia Guerra
PENCILLER

Jose Marzan Jr.
INKER

Lee Loughridge
COLORIST

LETTERER

COVER ARTIST

ASST. EDITOR

EDITOR

# Y: THE SCRIPT

The complete script to Y: THE LAST MAN #60
by co-creator and writer Brian K. Vaughan.

**"ALAS"**

The Full Script for Y #60

Prepared for Vertigo Comics

July 17, 2007

Brian K. Vaughan

## Page One

**Page One, Panel One**

We're somewhere outdoors on a sunny morning for this three-quarter SPLASH, a nice full-figure shot of a 22-YEAR-OLD YORICK BROWN (looking much like he did way back in our first issue). He's dressed in casual contemporary attire. Yorick smiles sheepishly as he gives us a little wave. He's standing next to his one piece of luggage.

1) Yorick: Um.
2) Yorick: Hey.

**Page One, Panel Two**

Cut over to who Yorick is speaking to, a new character named CATHERINE. This 25-year-old woman has short curly red hair and a constellation of FRECKLES dotting her attractive face. She's dressed entirely in black.

3) Catherine: Holy shit.
4) Catherine: You're... you're *him*, aren't you?

## Page Two

**Page Two, Panel One**

Pull out to a shot of both awkward young people.

1) Yorick: I guess so.
2) Yorick: And you must be *Catherine*.

3) Catherine: Jesus, my bosses at the Culper Sphere told me this was an important gig, but I had no idea it was *you*, uh... sire?

**Page Two, Panel Two**

Push in on Catherine, who's clearly still having trouble with all of this.

4) Catherine: No, wait. "Sir." Sir, right?
5) Catherine: I've never actually used that word before.

**Page Two, Panel Three**

Pull out to the largest panel of the page for a shot of both characters.

6) Yorick: Well, do me a favor and never use it again.

7) Catherine: Roger that.
8) Catherine: Apologies for being such a fuckin' fritz. This is just... strange.

**Page Two, Panel Four**

This is just a shot of young Yorick, as he finally reveals what the fuck is going on here:

9) Yorick: What, you've never met a clone before?

## Page Three

**Page Three, Panel One**

Cut back to Catherine, confused.

1) Catherine: Uh, pretty much *everyone* our age was cloned from somebody, right?

**Page Three, Panel Two**

Cut to Clone Yorick, who is every bit as un-smooth as his predecessor.

2) Yorick: No, I know. That's the joke.
3) Yorick: Women sometimes freak out because I'm usually the first *guy* they've ever seen in person, so I always say...

**Page Three, Panel Three**

Pull out to a shot of both characters, as Yorick picks up his bag.

4) Yorick: Sorry.
5) Yorick: Humor isn't my strong suit.

6) Catherine: Anyway, the President is waiting for you.

**Page Three, Panel Four**

Change angles on Catherine for this largest panel of the page, as she gestures behind her so that we can finally see what kind of vehicle brought her here. Parked in the immediate background is a SKYCAR, more of a near-futuristic horizontal/vertical-takeoff vehicle than a full-on *Jetsons*-style flying car, this aircraft definitely suggests that we're now in the FUTURE, a future where women have obviously made some significant advances. Feel free to use your imagination, Pia, but here are some sample contemporary models, just to help you keep this in the realm of the plausible: www.moller.com

7) Catherine: Might as well get this over with, huh?

## Page Four

**Page Four, SPLASH**

Hooray, this page is entirely black! Instead of one of our date/location captions, this final title card will be right in the center of this otherwise empty splash (and then you'll never have to letter one of these things again, Clem!).

1) White text in center of black splash (**same-sized font as usual, please!**):

**Paris, France**
**Sixty Years from Now**

**Pages Five and Six**

**Pages Five and Six, DOUBLE-PAGE SPREAD**

Okay, Pia, this is our first (and last) ever DOUBLE-PAGE SPREAD, a majestic skyline shot of PARIS CIRCA 2067 (the Eiffel Tower helps us get our bearings). Instead of towering phallic skyscrapers, the city now has SEVERAL SPHERICAL BUILDINGS with large HOLES in the center of them. These tall buildings arch high into the sky to clearly suggest a more VAGINAL kind of civil engineering. I'm picturing a much more overtly "feminine" version of the proposed EUROSCRAPER, so don't feel the need to be subtle about this at all, Pia!

Catherine's soaring SKYCAR is just a tiny craft in this shot, soaring over the city from our left to right, to help carry our eyes from page five to six...

No Copy

## Page Seven

**Page Seven, Panel One**

Smash cut to this close-up of a SIXTY-SOMETHING BETH JUNIOR, a grown-up version of the baby girl that *our* Yorick sired in that church with the scarred Beth II about a million issues ago. Beth Junior now has long white hair with a single streak of black in it. She looks troubled.

1) Assistant (from off): Beth?

**Page Seven, Panel Two**

Pull out to this largest panel of the page to reveal that we're in a stately office inside of what we will soon learn is the *Palais de l'Élysée*. Beth is staring out a window at nothing in particular as her ASSISTANT, a thirty-something East Indian woman in traditional attire, enters carrying a file folder.

2) Assistant: We have a situation, I'm afraid.

3) President Beth: Another India-Pakistan pissing match?

4) Assistant: No, this is more of a good news/bad news thing.

**Page Seven, Panel Three**

Push in close on the troubled assistant.

5) Assistant: Iran has the bomb.

**Page Seven, Panel Four**

Pull out, as "President Beth" spins around to confront her assistant.

6) President Beth: *Excuse me?*

7) Assistant: The one satellite we've got left confirms it.

8) President Beth: And how the hell is that good news?

## Page Eight

**Page Eight, Panel One**
Push in on the assistant, arching an eyebrow.

1) Assistant: Well, I'd say producing twenty-five kilograms of highly enriched uranium is a significant breakthrough...
2) Assistant: ... especially for a society where women weren't even allowed to *sing in public* before the Le Grand Départ struck.

**Page Eight, Panel Two**
Pull out to a shot of both women, as the assistant hands over her folder.

3) Assistant: The bad news, of course...

4) President Beth: Yes, "meet the new boss."
5) President Beth: We're going to need the Russians help to defuse the situation. I have to talk with *Vladimir.*

**Page Eight, Panel Three**
Change angles for this largest panel of the page, as Beth starts storming out of this room. The assistant follows at her heels. Please leave room for this exchange:

6) Assistant: The Czar? Beth, he's not exactly on speaking terms with the North Atlantic Sororité these days.

7) President Beth: Then we'll communicate through back channels. His mother used to help change my diapers for God's sake.

8) Assistant: But Ciba Weber died years ago.

9) President Beth: And remember the old Russian woman I introduced you to at her funeral? She still has Vlad's ear. We'll send a communiqué through her.

**Page Eight, Panel Four**
Push in closer on the two, as Beth cracks a smile.

10) Assistant: Natalya, right? Her English was excellent.

11) President Beth: Heh.

12) Assistant: What?

**Page Eight, Panel Five**
Push in on President Beth, as she turns to look back at "us."

13) President Beth: Long story.

14) Catherine (from off): *Mademoiselle la Présidente?*

## Page Nine

**Page Nine, Panel One**
Cut over to a gilded entryway in this majestic hallway, where Catherine is nervously introducing an equally apprehensive Yorick.

1) Catherine: *Excusez-moi.*
2) Catherine: *Est-ce que je peux me présenter—*

**Page Nine, Panel Two**
Cut back to Beth, as she dismissively hands her folder back to her assistant.

3) President Beth: It's all right, Catherine.
4) President Beth: I apparently possess just enough "Quality of Frenchman" that my country-women aren't threatened when I flirt with my native tongue.

**Page Nine, Panel Three**
Pull out to a shot of Beth, Catherine and Yorick, as the sixty-something President proudly takes young Yorick's hands in hers.

5) President Beth: Christ, will you look at those eyebrows?
6) President Beth: They were right about this one. It's like you're really him.

7) Yorick: Thank you, ma'am, but technically, I'm just lowly Yorick Brown the *Seventeenth*.

**Page Nine, Panel Four**
Finally, this shot of Beth can be the largest of the page. She's in the foreground of this low-angle upshot, and looming on the wall behind her, we can see a MASSIVE FRAMED PORTRAIT of a young BETH II (with that distinctive SCAR across her nose) holding her BABY GIRL, one of the last "conventional" births of the last sixty years.

8) President Beth: Yes, I'm well aware of the burdens of carrying another's name.

## Page Ten

**Page Ten, Panel One**
Cut over to Yorick, making uncomfortable small talk as he looks up at the off-panel painting.

1) Yorick: My surrogate gave me one of your mom's books on secular humanism.
2) Yorick: It was really... interesting.

**Page Ten, Panel Two**
Cut back to Beth, suddenly looking a little sad.

3) President Beth: Nice of you to say, but Beth Senior converted back to post-Vatican III Catholicism late in life.
4) President Beth: Atheism apparently loses its luster when the finish line approaches.

**Page Ten, Panel Three**
Pull out to the largest panel of the page for a shot of all three remaining characters (the assistant can be walking away in the background).

5) President Beth: Anyway, this isn't about my mother, it's about my *father*.
6) President Beth: The *first* Yorick Brown.

7) Yorick: I'm really sorry I never got to meet him. He died while I was still in quarantine, back when they weren't sure if we'd be affected by residual—

**Page Ten, Panel Four**
Push in on Beth, startlingly matter-of-fact:

8) President Beth: That's the thing, Yorick.
9) President Beth: My dad is still alive.

**Page Ten, Panel Five**
Cut over to Yorick and Catherine, both of whom are appropriately SHOCKED.

10) Yorick: Huh?

## Page Eleven

**Page Eleven, Panel One**
Change angles for this largest panel of the page, as Beth leads Yorick away from a stationary Catherine.

1) President Beth: He was a wonderful father, but his relationship with my mom was... complicated.
2) President Beth: Even from an early age, I knew they were really only staying together for me.

**Page Eleven, Panel Two**
Push in on Beth and Yorick, as they walk down this long hallway.

3) President Beth: No matter how well he tried to hide it, it was clear Dad was always in love with someone else.

4) Yorick: The other Beth, right?
5) Yorick: Beth Deville?

**Page Eleven, Panel Three**
Change angles on the two.

6) President Beth: That's what the shitty biopic would have you believe... but there was actually

another woman.

7) President Beth: I don't think he was ever the same after he lost her, and time only seemed to make the pain worse.

**Page Eleven, Panel Four**

Push in on the President, suddenly looking a little ashamed.

8) President Beth: On his most recent birthday, dad tried to kill himself.

**Page Eleven, Panel Five**

Pull out to another shot of this duo, as they turn a corner.

9) President Beth: With all the threats he'd been receiving from the Daughters of the Revolution, we decided to spin his hospitalization as "death by natural causes."

10) President Beth: He's been secretly committed here at the *Palais de l'Élysée* ever since.

11) Yorick: What do you mean *committed*?

## Page Twelve

**Page Twelve, Panel One**

Push in on President Beth, smiling at us pleasantly.

1) President Beth: Yorick, my dad wasn't always a melancholy man.

2) President Beth: He doesn't have much longer, and I'd like for him to laugh just once more before he goes.

**Page Twelve, Panel Two**

Pull out, as Beth and Yorick stop in front of an intimidating IRON DOOR.

3) President Beth: I have reason to believe you're just the man for that job.

4) Yorick: Me?

5) Yorick: Yeah, but... *no*.

**Page Twelve, Panel Three**

Change angles for this largest panel of the page, as Beth gently PUSHES Yorick through the now-open iron door.

6) President Beth: Trust me, just seeing you is going to remind him of happier times.

7) President Beth: All you have to do is be yourself.

**Page Twelve, Panel Four**

And now we're inside this dark room with the 22-year-old clone of Yorick, as the heavy door SLAMS SHUT behind him.

8) SFX: *WHAM*

**Page Twelve, Panel Five**

Push in tight on Yorick, as he scrunches up his nose like he smells something awful.

9) Another Voice (from off): Hn.

## Page Thirteen

**Page Thirteen, SPLASH**

Finally, cut over to what the off-panel Young Yorick sees, an 87-YEAR-OLD MAN sitting in a chair in the center of this room. He's wearing a STRAITJACKET. This is, of course, *our* Yorick Brown, looking a little like an older, balder, more disheveled version of his own grandfather (who we met briefly in a flashback at the opening of *Safeword*).

There's a BARRED WINDOW in the background of this dark room, empty except for the TWELVE CAPUCHIN HELPER MONKEYS scurrying about. One of these animals is sitting on Old Yorick's shoulder, gently brushing what's left of his wispy white hair.

1) Old Yorick: Did you know Elvis had a twin brother?

## Page Fourteen

**Page Fourteen, Panel One**

Young Yorick, like his predecessor so often was, is confused.

1) Yorick: ...

2) Yorick: Who's Elvis?

**Page Fourteen, Panel Two**
Push in tight on Old Yorick.

3) Old Yorick: Guy who could make women faint just by shaking his hips.
4) Old Yorick: He was a *real*...

**Page Fourteen, Panel Three**
Pull out to the largest panel of the page for a shot of both men. Monkeys SCURRY as Junior approaches Senior.

5) Old Yorick: Forget it. Their turn at the microphone now.
6) Old Yorick: So, you're my Ghost of Christmas Past, huh?

7) Yorick: Um, actually, it's July. And I'm not a ghost, I'm your genetic—

**Page Fourteen, Panel Four**
Push in on Old Yorick, still a bit of a wise-ass (though he's NOT smiling).

8) Old Yorick: I'm old, kid, not retarded.

**Page Fourteen, Panel Five**
Pull out to another shot of the duo.

9) Yorick: Oh.

10) Old Yorick: I suppose my overprotective baby girl told you I tried to off myself.
11) Old Yorick: Well, that's bullshit. It was just a... a *joke*. Because I was eighty-five and about to be eighty-sixed. Like the turn of phrase?

**Page Fourteen, Panel Six**
Now we're on just Young Yorick, a little horrified.

12) Yorick: Sounds hilarious.

## Page Fifteen

**Page Fifteen, Panel One**
Old Yorick squints at his off-panel clone.

1) Old Yorick: What's your story, junior?

**Page Fifteen, Panel Two**
Pull out to a shot of both men.

2) Yorick: My story?

3) Old Yorick: Another boring Bildungsroman, probably. You have a lady friend or what?

4) Yorick: Not yet. I haven't been a free man for that long. But I'm trying.

**Page Fifteen, Panel Three**
Push in on Young Yorick, smiling affably.

5) Yorick: It's like that old saying.
6) Yorick: We spend nine months trying to get out of a woman and the rest of our lives trying to get back in.

**Page Fifteen, Panel Four**
Cut back to Old Yorick, frowning with disappointment.

7) Old Yorick: Do yourself a spectacular favor and stow that fratboy horsecrap with a quickness.
8) Old Yorick: Girls aren't a game.

**Page Fifteen, Panel Five**
Pull out a bit for this largest panel of the page, a full-bleed shot with no panel borders. We're still on Old Yorick, but now the background behind him has suddenly CHANGED to that of an ARID DESERT.

9) Old Yorick: Not one that you can win.

## Page Sixteen

**Page Sixteen, Panel One**

Similar framing, but now Yorick has disappeared for this page-wide establishing shot of AFRICA'S KALAHARI DESERT.

No Copy

**Page Sixteen, Panel Two**

Change angles for this largest panel of the page, a nice shot of HERO BROWN who is now in her late thirties, roughly five years older than when we saw her last issue. *(We're obviously in the past, but let's PLEASE not use muted colors for these flashbacks. I know our audience is smart enough to tell when we're changing time periods without us chromatically holding their hands!)* Anyway, Hero is wearing a tank top but no bra, no longer trying to hide her missing breast/mastectomy scar. Oh, and she's carrying a big-ass HUNTING RIFLE.

1) Hero: Hello?

**Page Sixteen, Panel Three**

Push in on Hero, as she AIMS her rifle at a nearby large tree.

2) Hero: I can *hear* you, bitch.
3) Hero: Get your poaching ass out here before I blow it off.

**Page Sixteen, Panel Four**

Push in tighter on Hero, as her eyes go WIDE.

4) Another Voice (from off): Easy, Hero.

## Page Seventeen

**Page Seventeen, Panel One**

Cut over to what the off-panel Hero sees for this largest panel of the page, a big shot of a 32-YEAR-OLD YORICK BROWN, who has our ol' pal AMPERSAND on his shoulder. This young man is a little older, a little wiser and now COMPLETELY BALD. He looks about as good with a shaved head as we freakish bald bastards can. Yorick's got an Indiana Jones amount of face stubble, and appropriate desert attire. He has a glistening platinum WEDDING RING on his left hand.

1) Hero (from off): *Yorick?*

2) Ampersand: *eek*

**Page Seventeen, Panel Two**

Pull out to a shot of this former couple, as Hero slings her rifle over her shoulder.

3) Hero: What *happened* to you?

4) Yorick: Thanks, you look good, too.

5) Hero: You know what I mean. I thought you were trying to enjoy wedded bliss with *Other* Beth. What the hell are you doing in the Kalahari? 'Cause if you're looking for *closure...*

**Page Seventeen, Panel Three**

Push in on Yorick, as he pulls out Agent 355's (unextended) COLLAPSIBLE BATON.

6) Yorick: No, stopped looking for that a long time ago.
7) Yorick: Just wanted to bring something I forgot to give you at Mom's ceremony.

**Page Seventeen, Panel Four**

Pull out to a shot of both characters, as Hero looks down at the baton in her hands, which she's EXTENDING here.

8) Hero: What is it?

9) Yorick: Something I got from a friend of mine.
10) Yorick: Figured you'd be less likely to shoot your eye out with it while you're out here doing your whole "white woman's burden" thing.

## Page Eighteen

**Page Eighteen, Panel One**

Change angles on Hero, as she looks out at the vast wasteland.

1) Hero: Thanks, but it's not like that.
2) Hero: The last of the lionesses need our protection, but these women don't need a goddamn thing.

**Page Eighteen, Panel Two**
Pull out to a shot of both characters for this largest panel of the page. Hero is looking out at us in the foreground, as Yorick listens on in the background.

3) Hero: Everyone thought of the "bushmen" as primitive, but they treated their wives and daughters as equals about 20,000 years before the rest of the planet even considered the idea.
4) Hero: When all the boys died, the San women just divided the hunting and gathering duties amongst themselves.

**Page Eighteen, Panel Three**
Push in on Hero, as she turns back around to look at us.

5) Hero: They did what we all did, really. They adapted. They evolved.
6) Hero: They moved on.

**Page Eighteen, Panel Four**
And this is just a nice shot of Yorick, trying to put on a happy face.

7) Yorick: Wow, you're even starting to *sound* like her.

**Page Eighteen, Panel Five**
Pull out, as Ampersand LEAPS back to Yorick.

8) Hero: Sorry.
9) Hero: She'll actually be back soon if you want to—

10) Yorick: Thanks, but Ampersand and I should probably hit the road. We have a lot to do, and I want to be back for my little one's eighth birthday party.

## Page Nineteen

**Page Nineteen, Panel One**
Change angles on the group.

1) Hero: Where are you gentlemen off to next?

2) Yorick: Wales, believe it or not. I'm taking a month off to do a little research for my first novel.

3) Hero: Seriously? What's it about?

**Page Nineteen, Panel Two**
Push in on Yorick, but please leave room for his book pitch:

4) Yorick: I don't know yet. But there's this old Welsh custom I read about. The Melltith, they called it. Thought it might make for good historical fiction.
5) Yorick: Apparently, wedding parties would chop down trees and start fires and come up with all sorts of crazy obstacles to stop the groom from getting to his bride on the big day. It was supposed to prove a man's worth, I guess.

**Page Nineteen, Panel Three**
Pull out to one last shot of the duo. Hero smiles knowingly, but Yorick is oblivious.

6) Hero: You really think that's all it was for, Yorick?

7) Yorick: How do you mean?

8) Another Voice (from behind Hero): Hero?

**Page Nineteen, Panel Four**
Push in on Hero, as she turns around to look behind her.

9) Hero: Cool, here she comes.
10) Hero: Be nice for you two to at least say...

**Page Nineteen, Panel Five**
Pull out to the largest panel of the page, as Hero turns around to see that Yorick and Ampersand have once again DISAPPEARED, as they so often do.

11) Hero: ... hello?

12) Another Voice (from off): You all right?

## Page Twenty

**Page Twenty, Panel One**

Cut over to a concerned BETH DEVILLE for this largest panel of the page. Now in her early thirties, the tanned and fit Beth is looking lovely as ever in casual civilian attire. She's carrying a cloth sling over her shoulder filled with some kind of local nuts.

1) Beth Deville: I thought that homeopathic stuff I found was helping with your voices.

**Page Twenty, Panel Two**

Cut back to a smiling Hero, as she tucks away her baton.

2) Hero: Just singing to myself, Beth.

**Page Twenty, Panel Three**

Push in tight on a smiling Beth.

3) Beth Deville: Whew. Excited about dinner?
4) Beth Deville: I believe Team Deville/Brown is closing in on the record for most mongongo nuts ever consumed by two—

**Page Twenty, Panel Four**

Pull out, as Hero PULLS Beth close to her. They're smiling as they stare into each other's eyes with a familiar comfort.

5) Hero: Hasn't anyone ever told you that women should be seen and not heard?

6) Beth Deville: I thought that was children.

7) Hero: Whatever...

**Page Twenty, Panel Five**

Push in closer for this full-bleed panel, as the two women PASSIONATELY KISS. It's evolution, of a sort.

No Copy

## Page Twenty-one

**Page Twenty-one, Panel One**

Smash cut back to the future for this silent close-up of Old Yorick, lost in thought.

No Copy

**Page Twenty-one, Panel Two**

Pull out to the largest panel of the page for this shot of both men, as Young Yorick listens to his straitjacketed elder.

1) Old Yorick: So, you moving here or what?

2) Yorick: To Gay Paree?
3) Yorick: No, I'm thinking about relocating to Canada. I'm interested in law, and one of my brothers told me the University of Ottawa might be open to enrolling a male student.

**Page Twenty-one, Panel Three**

Push in closer on the two.

4) Old Yorick: Well, don't forget your English in that bilingual wasteland.
5) Old Yorick: A whole country of women, and one little boy still magically transforms "elles" into "ils." It's like I told her when we met, *Français* is for chauvinists.

6) Yorick: Wait, told who?

**Page Twenty-one, Panel Four**

This is just a shot of Old Yorick, as he begins to VIOLENTLY COUGH.

7) Old Yorick: It doesn't really—
8) Old Yorick: *-HKK- -koff- -koff- -koff- -hkk-*

## Page Twenty-two

**Page Twenty-two, Panel One**

Young Yorick quickly THROWS OPEN the heavy barred window, letting more fresh air and sunlight stream in through this glassless opening. We can see a nice view of Paris from this fourth floor.

1) Yorick: Hold on.
2) Yorick: I'll... I'll get you some fresh air.

**Page Twenty-two, Panel Two**

Cut back to Old Yorick, who closes his eyes and takes a deep breath as the SUNLIGHT hits his face.

3) Old Yorick: hhh.

**Page Twenty-two, Panel Three**

Pull out to the largest panel of the page for a shot of both men.

4) Old Yorick: You said you had brothers.
5) Old Yorick: The rest of them all like you? Like us?

6) Yorick: DNA-wise, you mean? No, they finally started engineering new strains last year.

**Page Twenty-two, Panel Four**

Push in on Old Yorick, lost in thought.

7) Old Yorick: "New strains."
8) Old Yorick: Like a disease.

**Page Twenty-two, Panel Five**

Push in even tighter on Old Yorick, for this extreme close-up of just HIS EYES, faded and spotted with cataracts.

9) Old Yorick: About right.

## Page Twenty-three

**Page Twenty-three, Panel One**

Cut into the past for this similar close-up of eyes, but these eyes are younger, and seen through the glare of a pair of EYEGLASSES.

No Copy

**Page Twenty-three, Panel Two**

Pull out to the largest panel of the page to reveal that we're looking at a 45-YEAR-OLD YORICK, who's still bald, but now clean-shaven. He's wearing a smart pair of rimless eyeglasses, and he has an OLDER AMPERSAND on his shoulder. This mature Yorick is now wandering through a stark, white, Kubrickian LABORATORY.

1) Yorick: Doc?

**Page Twenty-three, Panel Three**

Push in closer on the man.

2) Yorick: Dr. Mann?

**Page Twenty-three, Panel Four**

Change angles on Yorick, as he rounds a corner.

3) Yorick: Don't make me say "Allison."
4) Yorick: I still can't bring myself to call you—

5) Another Voice (from off): Hello, Yorick.

## Page Twenty-four

**Page Twenty-four, Panel One**

Cut over to ROSE for this largest panel of the page. The forty-something Australian woman still has her trademark EYEPATCH, but we can now see that she's SEVERAL MONTHS PREGNANT. Sadly, she's wearing the all-black attire of a woman who's just attended a FUNERAL.

1) Rose: Thanks for coming, mate.

**Page Twenty-four, Panel Two**

Cut back to Yorick, heartbroken.

2) Yorick: Oh, no.
3) Yorick: Am... am I too late?

**Page Twenty-four, Panel Three**

And this is just a shot of Rose, as a single tear rolls out of her one good eye.

No Copy

**Page Twenty-four, Panel Four**

Pull out, as the two old friends EMBRACE.

4) Yorick: I'm sorry, Rose.
5) Yorick: I'm so sorry.

6) Rose: She tried to hold on for you... for *both* of you.

## Page Twenty-five

**Page Twenty-five, Panel One**

Change angles on the two, as Yorick feels Rose's swollen belly.

1) Yorick: So this is really... ?

2) Rose: The first of many, hopefully.
3) Rose: Took her ages to make a copy of you that Ampersand's brood would *inoculate* instead of annihilate, but I think we have a winner.

4) Ampersand: *urn*

**Page Twenty-five, Panel Two**

Push in closer.

5) Yorick: But how are *you*?

6) Rose: I'm... I'll find a way to soldier on.
7) Rose: And even if I don't, someone else will carry her torch.

**Page Twenty-five, Panel Three**

Pull out for this largest panel of the page. We're down in a sealed laboratory with SEVERAL CLONES OF DR. MANN (varying in age from 17 to 23). These young women are all dressed differently, but the eldest is wearing a WHITE LAB COAT. She's having an argument with one of her punk-attired rebellious younger "sisters" in the foreground of this low-angle upshot. High in the background above and behind them, we can see Yorick and Rose looking down at this scene through the glass of a second-floor observation deck overlooking this lab.

8) Rose: No worries there.

## Page Twenty-six

**Page Twenty-six, Panel One**

Push in on Rose and an awestruck Yorick, as they look down through the glass at the off-panel clones.

1) Yorick: "Dr. Men."

2) Rose: They're young, but smart.
3) Rose: The eldest already helped the Hartle twins solve the livestock crisis back in the States.

**Page Twenty-six, Panel Two**

Push in on Yorick, whose eyes begin to well with tears.

4) Yorick: They all talk with their hands just like she did.
5) Yorick: It's... it's kind of beautiful.

**Page Twenty-six, Panel Three**

Pull out to the largest panel of the page, as Rose pulls out a SMALL GLASS MICROSCOPE SLIDE. Yorick looks at it with confusion as he wipes his tears away.

6) Rose: Which reminds me.
7) Rose: She wanted you to see this.

8) Yorick: A lock of hair? Don't tell me she cured baldness on the way out, too.

**Page Twenty-six, Panel Four**
And this is a dramatic close-up of Rose.

9) Rose: Yorick.
10) Rose: She took it off Agent 355.

**Page Twenty-six, Panel Five**
Cut to Yorick, almost too stunned for words.

11) Yorick (**small font**, a whisper): What?

## Page Twenty-seven

**Page Twenty-seven, Panel one**
Pull out to a shot of both characters.

1) Rose: Ali always knew how much she meant to you.
2) Rose: And ever since we started cloning females en masse, we've have the wherewithal to "bring back," for lack of a better phrase, any woman, living or—

3) Yorick: No.

**Page Twenty-seven, Panel Two**
Push in closer on the two.

4) Yorick: Thank you, but no.
5) Yorick: I... I wouldn't want that.

6) Rose: No offense, luv, but it's not all about you. What if Three-fifty wanted to...

**Page Twenty-seven, Panel Three**
This is just a shot of Yorick and Ampersand, as they both STARE DAGGERS at us.

No Copy

**Page Twenty-seven, Panel Four**
Cut back to Rose, who's obviously not going to push this.

7) Rose: Right then.

**Page Twenty-seven, Panel Five**
And finally, we close with this close-up of Ampersand, who's clearly started to AGE.

8) Rose (from just off): Say no more.

## Page Twenty-eight

**Page Twenty-eight, Panel One**
Smash cut back to the future for this close-up of a YOUNGER CAPUCHIN MONKEY.

1) Monkey: *ahk*

**Page Twenty-eight, Panel Two**
Pull out to reveal that this is the monkey sitting on the shoulder of the straitjacketed OLD YORICK.

2) Old Yorick: Took 'em long enough.

**Page Twenty-eight, Panel Three**
Pull out to the largest panel of the page for a shot of both men.

3) Yorick: To start making other guys, you mean? Well, they've had trouble with the Y-chromosome, apparently.

4) Old Yorick: That's because cloning is *crap*.
5) Old Yorick: You can photocopy Mann's brain as many times as you want, but without her asshole dad pushing those girls every step of the way, you'll never have her *mind*.

**Page Twenty-eight, Panel Four**
Cut over to an annoyed Young Yorick, giving the old man a taste of his own shit.

6) Yorick: To be honest, right about now, I'm really thankful for the whole nature-nurture divide.

**Page Twenty-eight, Panel Five**
Cut to Old Yorick. He's not smiling, but he's at least impressed with this kid's chutzpah.

7) Old Yorick (**small font**, under his breath): That a boy.

## Page Twenty-nine

**Page Twenty-nine, Panel One**
Pull out to the largest panel of the page, as Young Yorick watches one of the helper monkeys fetch PILLS from a nearby shelf.

1) Yorick: Whoa.
2) Yorick: These little guys are so well behaved.

**Page Twenty-nine, Panel Two**
Cut over to Old Yorick, as one of the monkeys carefully feeds him his pill.

3) Old Yorick: Tell me about it.
4) Old Yorick: A hundred monkeys later and they still haven't gotten him right.

**Page Twenty-nine, Panel Three**
Pull out to a shot of both men, as the monkeys scamper away from Old Yorick.

5) Yorick: Sorry?

6) Old Yorick: Yeah.

**Page Twenty-nine, Panel Four**
This is just a surreal close-up of Old Yorick. As the background behind him turns BLINDINGLY WHITE, we can suddenly see the old man's BREATH, as if the temperature in his cell just dropped below freezing.

7) Old Yorick: Me, too.

## Page Thirty

**Page Thirty, Panel One**
Cut into the past for this thin letterbox panel that's ENTIRELY WHITE.

No Copy

**Page Thirty, Panel Two**
We can now tell that this whiteness is a SNOW FLURRY, as a FIGURE cuts through this blizzard. It's a 60-YEAR OLD YORICK, who now has a trim WHITE BEARD to go with his glasses. He's wearing a cool hat, a black trenchcoat, and a familiar GREEN SCARF that flutters in the wind.

1) Yorick: Don't worry, buddy.

**Page Thirty, Panel Three**
Pull out to the largest panel of the page, as we reveal that Yorick is cradling a FORTY-SOMETHING AMPERSAND, who is clearly gray and frail with age. (Capuchins rarely live past forty-five... though there are exceptions, True Believers, so don't give up hope yet.) Anyway, they're trekking through a beautifully snow-blanketed forest.

2) Yorick: Everything's going to be okay.

3) Ampersand: *cff*

## Page Thirty-one

**Page Thirty-one, Panel One**
Push in on Yorick.

1) Yorick: I know it's hard, but you'll be all better soon.
2) Yorick: We're going to visit an old friend. You always liked her, remember?

**Page Thirty-one, Panel Two**
Push in on the gray-maned Ampersand, who can barely keep his eyes open.

3) Ampersand: *fff*

**Page Thirty-one, Panel Three**
Pull out to the largest panel of the page for a shot of both males. Yorick reaches into his pocket as he trudges through the snow.

4) Yorick: You hungry?
5) Yorick: Okay, pal, here we go.

**Page Thirty-one, Panel Four**
Push in, as Yorick tries in vain to feed a grape to his ailing friend.

6) Ampersand: *tk*

7) Yorick: Come on, dummy.
8) Yorick: You love grapes.

**Page Thirty-one, Panel Five**
This is just a close-up of Yorick, desperate and afraid.

9) Yorick: Please eat.

## Page Thirty-two

**Page Thirty-two, Panel One**
Push in on Ampersand, as he reluctantly bites into the purple grape.

No Copy

**Page Thirty-two, Panel Two**
Cut back to Yorick, smiling with a bit of relief.

1) Yorick: Thanks.

**Page Thirty-two, Panel Three**
Pull out to a shot of both friends for this largest panel of the page, as Yorick stops in his tracks.

2) Yorick: Remember Brazil?
3) Yorick: When those roller derby psychos had me tied up, and you started screaming at the top of your lungs when I tried to get out?

**Page Thirty-two, Panel Four**
Push in on Yorick, as he begins to cry.

4) Yorick: You have been one piece of shit pet.

**Page Thirty-two, Panel Five**
Push in on Amp, as he uncomfortably FOAMS AT THE MOUTH.

5) Ampersand: *tsss*

## Page Thirty-three

**Page Thirty-three, Panel One**
Pull out to a shot of the two, as Yorick (still cradling Ampersand) falls to his knees.

1) Yorick: Ah, fuck.

**Page Thirty-three, Panel Two**
Push in on Yorick, clearly pained with guilt.

2) Yorick: Why the fuck did I do that?

**Page Thirty-three, Panel Three**
Pull out for this largest panel of the page. Yorick gently wipes off Ampersand's mouth as the snow swirls around them.

3) Yorick: They said it wouldn't hurt, Amp. I... I didn't want you to hurt anymore.
4) Yorick: They promised it would be quick.

**Page Thirty-three, Panel Four**
Push in on Ampersand, as he looks up with eyes that seem apologetic. Loving, even.

No Copy

**Page Thirty-three, Panel Five**
Cut up to Yorick, smiling through tears.

5) Yorick: Yeah.
6) Yorick: I know.

**Page Thirty-three, Panel Six**
On Ampersand, as he finally closes his eyes.

7) Yorick (from off): I know.

## Page Thirty-four

**Page Thirty-four, SPLASH**
Finally, cut BEHIND the kneeling Yorick, hunched over the animal we can't see, but which Yorick is still cradling. As the snow dies down a little, we can now see that Yorick has stopped in front of a LARGE OAK TREE. Carved high in the bark of this makeshift tombstone is an old message that has not faded with age:

**355**
**PEACE**

## Page Thirty-five

**Page Thirty-five, Panel One**
Smash cut back to the future for this largest panel of the page, a profile shot of Old Yorick and his young clone, as the two men stare at each other in silence.

No Copy

**Page Thirty-five, Panel Two**
Push in closer on the two.

1) Yorick: So this is it, huh?

2) Old Yorick: What's that?

3) Yorick: You know, growing old. All I have to look forward to is pain and misery and... and heartbreak.

**Page Thirty-five, Panel Three**
This is just a shot of Old Yorick, giving this some thought.

No Copy

**Page Thirty-five, Panel Four**
Similar framing, but now the old man looks up at us.

4) Old Yorick: No.
5) Old Yorick: No, first comes *boyhood.* You get to play with soldiers and spacemen, cowboys and ninjas, pirates and robots.
6) Old Yorick: But before you know it, all that comes to an end.

**Page Thirty-five, Panel Five**
Similar framing one more time.

7) Old Yorick: And then, Remo Williams, is when the adventure begins.

## Page Thirty-six

**Page Thirty-six, Panel One**
Cut to Young Yorick, dismayed about his existence.

1) Yorick: I have no idea what you're talking about.
2) Yorick: My life has been a total waste so far, and I'm *already* an adult!

**Page Thirty-six, Panel Two**
Cut to Old Yorick, arching an eyebrow.

3) Old Yorick: ...
4) Old Yorick: How old are you?

**Page Thirty-six, Panel Three**
Cut back to Young Yorick, looking just as boyish as our hero did way back in our first issue.

5) Yorick: Twenty-two.

**Page Thirty-six, Panel Four**
Cut back to Old Yorick, looking stolid.

No Copy

**Page Thirty-six, Panel Five**
Identical framing for this largest panel of the page, but now, for the first time in a decade, the old man SMILES.

No Copy

## Page Thirty-seven

**Page Thirty-seven, Panel One**
Cut to Young Yorick, clearly offended.

1) Yorick: What?

**Page Thirty-seven, Panel Two**
Pull out to a shot of both men for this largest panel of the page, as the monkeys begin to GATHER around a nervous Young Yorick.

2) Old Yorick: I turned your age a few weeks before the Plague hit, back when my life was even more of a mess than it is now.
3) Old Yorick: I was jobless, behind on rent, my girl was gone...

4) Yorick: Um, are your monkeys okay?

**Page Thirty-seven, Panel Three**
Push in on the straitjacketed Old Yorick.

5) Old Yorick: And my old man writes me this birthday note that says:
6) Old Yorick: "A pair of deuces ain't much... but sometimes, it can be a winning hand."

**Page Thirty-seven, Panel Four**
Cut to Young Yorick, as the monkeys SWARM him, climbing all over his body.

7) Yorick: Are... are they supposed to be doing this?

**Page Thirty-seven, Panel Five**
Cut back to the straitjacketed Old Yorick.

8) Old Yorick: You'll be fine, 'Rick.
9) Old Yorick: Just go out there and get your heart broken in, so it'll be ready when you really need it.

## Page Thirty-eight

**Page Thirty-eight, Panel One**
Cut back to Young Yorick, as he BRUSHES the monkeys off of him.

1) Yorick: Hey!
2) Yorick: Call them off, would you?! They're gonna claw the eyes right out of my...

**Page Thirty-eight, Panel Two**
Pull out to the largest panel of the page, as Yorick looks up to see that his older self has seemingly DISAPPEARED, leaving only an EMPTY CHAIR in his place.

No Copy

**Page Thirty-eight, Panel Three**
Push in on a troubled Young Yorick.

3) Yorick: Yorick?

**Page Thirty-eight, Panel Four**

Change angles, as Yorick spots the window that *he* foolishly opened.

4) Yorick: No.

**Page Thirty-eight, Panel Five**
Cut outside for this low-angle upshot, as we look up at a distraught Young Yorick, who is looking out the window down at us far below. We can see the blue sky above him in the distant background.

No Copy

**Page Thirty-eight, Panel Six**
Tilt up more for this final page-wide letterbox panel, just a shot of that same blue sky.

5) Yorick (from off): *NO!*

## Page Thirty-nine

**Page Thirty-nine, Panel One**
This is an identical page-wide letterbox panel of blue sky.

No Copy

**Page Thirty-nine, Panel Two**
But now we TILT DOWN to this largest panel of the page to find that we're in the past (about six months after the Plague), looking at the WRECKAGE OF A MASSIVE 747, which is scattered over a beautiful summer field somewhere in the Northeast United States.

No Copy

**Page Thirty-nine, Panel Three**
Push in on the wreckage for this shot of a BADLY DECOMPOSED TIE-WEARING BUSINESSMAN, still belted into his seat.

1) A Voice (from off): Ouch!

## Page Forty

**Page Forty, Panel One**
Cut over to OUR 22-YEAR-OLD YORICK (circa somewhere between Issues #6 and 7), as he winces in pain like the pussy he is.

1) Yorick: I thought you were supposed to be a doctor!

**Page Forty, Panel Two**
Pull out to the largest panel of the page for this shot of Yorick and DR. MANN, who is patiently removing a SHARD OF DEBRIS from the bottom of Yorick's bare foot. Yorick and Ampersand are sitting on a piece of the plane's broken wing.

2) Dr. Mann: I am, unless my board certification expired with the board.

3) Yorick: Whatever, just start doing no harm already!

4) Dr. Mann: Why did you run barefoot into a debris field anyway?

**Page Forty, Panel Three**
Push in closer on the two, as Mann mutters under her breath.

5) Yorick: Because I thought there'd be peanuts, not a sea of rusty nails!
6) Yorick: And now I've probably got lockjaw!

7) Dr. Mann (**small font**, an aside): We should be so lucky.

**Page Forty, Panel Four**
Change angles, as a stolid Mann walks away from the petulant young Yorick.

8) Yorick: You won't be laughing when I catch up with the rest of these guys.

9) Dr. Mann: I'm off to look for a first-aid kit.
10) Dr. Mann: Don't put any pressure on that thing.

**Page Forty, Panel Five**
Push in on Yorick (with Ampersand on his shoulder), as the young man looks down at the WEDDING RING he keeps around his neck.

11) Ampersand: *glrt*

12) Yorick: Fuckin' A.

13) Another Voice (from off): Hey.

## Page Forty-one

**Page Forty-one, Panel One**

For this page-tall VERTICAL panel, cut over to AGENT 355, looking young and vibrant in this full-figure shot, the largest of the page. The sun is at her back, making a bit of a halo behind her head as she's dramatically backlit.

1) Agent 355: You okay?

**Page Forty-one, Panel Two**

Cut back to a frowning Yorick.

2) Yorick: No thanks to you.
3) Yorick: I thought you were supposed to be my guardian angel. Where the hell have you been?

**Page Forty-one, Panel Three**

Cut back to 355, as she holds up a bag of AIRPLANE PEANUTS.

4) Agent 355: Getting you these.

**Page Forty-one, Panel Four**

Pull out, as 355 sits down next to Yorick.

5) Yorick: Ah.

6) Agent 355: Uh-huh.

## Page Forty-two

**Page Forty-two, Panel One**

Push in on Yorick, looking worried for his life.

1) Yorick: Do you believe in heaven?

**Page Forty-two, Panel Two**

Pull out to a shot of both characters, as Yorick struggles to open his peanuts.

2) Agent 355: Jesus, you're not gonna *die*.

3) Yorick: Maybe, maybe not.
4) Yorick: I'm just curious.

**Page Forty-two, Panel Three**

Push in closer on the two friends, as Ampersand jumps over to 355.

5) Agent 355: Like, do I think there's life after death?
6) Agent 355: I hope not.

7) Yorick: But, didn't you say all of your family is dead? Wouldn't you want to see them again?

**Page Forty-two, Panel Four**

Change angles, as 355 takes the peanuts from Yorick.

8) Agent 355: Yeah, that'd be nice. For a while. But then...
9) Agent 355: Nah, I hope this is the end of the line.

10) Yorick: Why?

**Page Forty-two, Panel Five**

Push in on 355, as she nonchalantly OPENS the peanuts.

11) Agent 355: Why not?

**Page Forty-two, Panel Six**

Cut back to Yorick, who's being more Yorick than ever:

12) Yorick: Okay, think of a card, but don't tell me what it is yet.

## Page Forty-three

**Page Forty-three, Panel One**
Cut to 355, perplexed.

1) Agent 355: You are a strange kid.

**Page Forty-three, Panel Two**
Cut to Yorick, excited.

2) Yorick: Got it?
3) Yorick: It's the Queen of Hearts, right?

**Page Forty-three, Panel Three**
Pull out for a shot of both characters, as Amp returns to Yorick.

4) Agent 355: Not even close.
5) Agent 355: Six of clubs.

6) Yorick: Seriously? Damn. Every woman I've ever met has said Queen of Hearts.

**Page Forty-three, Panel Four**
Push in on 355, smiling.

7) Agent 355: You may need to meet more women.

**Page Forty-three, Panel Five**
Pull way out to this largest panel of the page, a full-bleed shot with no panel borders. 355 and Yorick can just be tiny figures amidst the wreckage.

8) Yorick: ha ha.

## Page Forty-four

**Page Forty-four, Panel One**
Smash cut back to the future for this close-up of an outraged PRESIDENT BETH.

1) President Beth: *What?*

**Page Forty-four, Panel Two**
Pull out to the largest panel of the page to reveal that we're back in Old Yorick's cell. The monkeys are running around everywhere, and their master's chair is still empty. Young Yorick is being interrogated by President Beth, her East Indian Assistant, and Catherine.

2) Yorick: I'm sorry, ma'am.
3) Yorick: I... I only took my eyes off him for a second.

**Page Forty-four, Panel Three**
Push in on a troubled Catherine.

4) Catherine: He *jumped?*

**Page Forty-four, Panel Four**
And this is a nice shot of Young Yorick, as a MONKEY climbs onto his shoulder. A cool breeze blows in through the open window behind him.

5) Yorick: No.

## Page Forty-five

**Page Forty-five, SPLASH**
Cut outside for this SPLASH, a nice exterior shot of this section of the *Palais de l'Élysée* (maybe we can spot some of the Eiffel Tower in the distance). We can see the ground and all four stories of this building, but Yorick's body is thankfully NOWHERE TO BE SEEN. Clearly, he didn't commit suicide. But where the fuck is he...?

1) From Window: He escaped.

## Page Forty-six

**Page Forty-six, Panel One**

Cut outside the Palace Gates, as two FEMALE FRENCH POLICE OFFICERS speak with each other.

No Copy

**Page Forty-six, Panel Two**

Cut onto the streets, as SEVERAL FEMALE CYCLISTS ride their bikes to and from work.

No Copy

**Page Forty-six, Panel Three**

Cut onto a nearby sidewalk, as a WOMAN walks hand in hand with her two YOUNG GIRLS (clones of herself, naturally). The wind is blowing their hair.

No Copy

## Page Forty-seven

**Page Forty-seven, Panel One**

Cut into a busy French marketplace, as FEMALE SHOPPERS buy goods from FEMALE VENDORS.

No Copy

**Page Forty-seven, Panel Two**

Cut into a nearby park, where SEVERAL YOUNG WOMEN are playing soccer in a park.

No Copy

**Page Forty-seven, Panel Three**

Cut outside a nearby office building, where BUSINESSWOMEN hold their dresses down as they step out onto the blustery street. A RANDOM WOMAN in this shot is looking up at something above her, just off-panel.

No Copy

## Page Forty-eight

**Page Forty-eight, Panel One**

And finally, this is just a shot of Old Yorick's EMPTY STRAITJACKET, which flutters in the wind as it's blown high into the sky. All we can see in the background are clouds. Naturally, as it's lifted into the air, the arms of the straitjacket reach for the heavens, forming a perfect letter "Y."

No Copy

**Page Forty-eight, Panel Two**

Let's put our title and closing credits into an insert panel at the very bottom of this page, much like the end of Y #58. Clem should definitely handle our last title, but rather than lettering our names, I thought that each of us should sign our *signatures* next to our credits. A final farewell from the whole team.

1) Title:

**ALAS**

2) Credits:

Brian K. Vaughan - Writer
Pia Guerra - Penciller
José Marzán, Jr.- Inker
Zylonol - Colorist
Clem Robins - Letterer
Massimo Carnevale - Cover Artist
Casey Seijas - Assistant Editor
Will Dennis - Editor